AF700720

THE *EVOLVING* NEW ECONOMY

By:

Douglas N. Thompson

Contributors:

Phillip M. Thompson
Christy A. Holt
Garry K. Ottosen
Joseph S. Peery

Published by Crossroads Research Institute, a nonprofit
operating foundation conducting research
on economic issues.

Crossroads Research Institute
807 E. South Temple
Salt Lake City, Utah 84102

Trustees:
Douglas N. Thompson
Joseph S. Peery
Garry K. Ottosen

Copyright © 2004 by Crossroads Research Institute
All Rights Reserved

ISBN: 0-9624038-3-0

For Catherine

CONTENTS

IT'S REALLY HAPPENING!

The evolving New Economy is being driven by the learning process. Two powerful but under-appreciated learning episodes are dramatically improving the economic outlook in the United States and throughout the world.

In the United States we have recently learned much about how to manage the environment in which the market system operates, especially the management of aggregate demand and of the intensity of structural competition. As a consequence we are now close to achieving the goal of an *average* unemployment rate as low as 4 percent.

Outside the United States, governments of countries containing considerably more than half the world's population have recently learned that they must adopt a market-managed economic system in order to modernize. The transition in many cases is going rapidly. To modernize they must obtain large amounts of capital. As a consequence they are now engaged in a vigorous competition with one another to improve their economic environments to attract the necessary capital investment. That under-appreciated competition is forcing radical changes upon many countries. It will likely be the most powerful force directing the evolution of the twenty-first century. Chapters 7 and 8 describe the many beneficial by-products of this vigorous competition.

This is an optimistic book. Every glint of optimism is based on faith in the learning process: what we have learned, the speed with which we are learning, and *an appraisal of the competitive pressures forcing us to continue to learn.* People and governments have learned and are continuing to learn at accelerating speed. Pessimists generally seem to believe that we will not learn. Learning comes through problem solving, and remarkable improvements in the world's problem-solving ability have occurred in just the past fifteen years.

We must continue the learning process. In this book we describe the next steps the U.S. government must take—steps that will allow us to achieve that 4 percent unemployment rate coexistent with low inflation and a high productivity growth rate. Chapters 1 and 2 describe the measures the government must take in order to maintain adequate demand. Chapter 3 explains the government's obligation to keep structural competition sufficiently intense to maintain low inflation, and Chapter 4 describes specific threats to the government's ability to do this and how these threats can be overcome. Chapters 6 and 7 forecast the remarkable effects that the New Economy will have on the entire world. Finally, the Appendix describes the impact of the New Economy on stock and bond performance.

We must continue to leave behind the bad ideas that have shackled past economic performance. We must not view the "business cycle" as an inevitable, self-generating feature of a capitalist economy in whose uncontrollable swings we are trapped. We can and will do better.

During the despondent days of 2002 after the stock market crash and during the meager recovery from the 2001 recession, we wrote a book entitled *The* Real *New Economy*. At that time most people spoke disparagingly of the so-called New Economy that had received so much attention in the late 1990s but that was based largely on stock speculation and Internet hype. We argued that we do, indeed, have a brilliant, long-lasting New Economy that will provide high growth in productivity and low average unemployment.

We mailed that book to all members of the American Economic Association and the National Association of Business Economists. We have been asked to clarify and expand some of the topics we passed over lightly in that book. We do so in this volume.

Chapter 1

SOLVING THE UNEMPLOYMENT PROBLEM

Sometimes monetary policy cannot adequately stimulate demand and economic activity, even when used aggressively. The recession and slow recovery of 2001–3 was such a time. There will surely be similar episodes in the future. What should be done? We suggest that a *flexible* fiscal stimulus plan can be an excellent solution. It is probably the *only* solution.

The 2001 to 2004 Employment Shortfall

In the two and a half years following the onset of the 2001 recession, unemployment in the United States rose by about 2.8 million. In addition, we lost the normal growth of more than three million workers we should have had over that same period. (The labor force typically grows about 1 percent a year.) Many discouraged workers dropped out of the labor force or failed to enter it. In total, employment in the middle of 2003 was five to six million below where it should have been. By late 2004 employment had still not recovered to its prerecession high; it was still almost six million below potential. We lost nearly four years of employment growth, as Chart 1.1 shows. We lost about twenty million worker-years of employment during the four-year period, and we will lose many more before we return to full employment. By historical standards the recession (even with a slow recovery) was mild. But that is not good enough. *We cannot let historical performance set the standard for the future. We must continue the learning process. We can do better*. The 2001–4 experience calls for a fundamental change in the way we deal with recessions and periods of slow growth.

What went wrong in that long drawn-out recessionary period? Aggregate demand (spending by consumers, businesses, and governments) was clearly *inadequate*. Spending is the initiator of economic activity. It activates the placing of orders, the hiring of workers, and the paying out of income. When it is inadequate we have recessions or periods of slow growth.

Chart 1.1 The Employment Shortfall
Nonfarm Employment in Millions

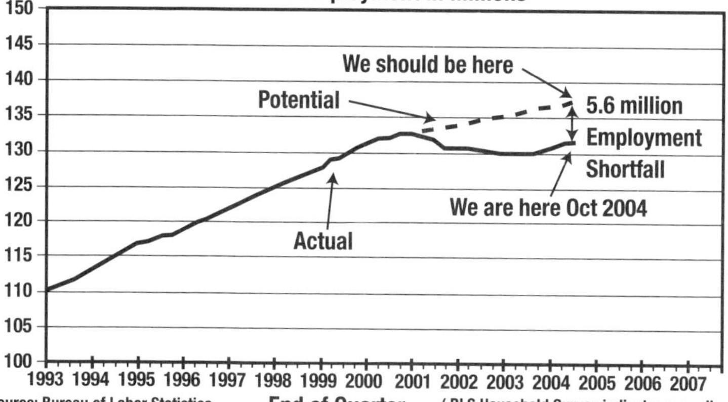

Source: Bureau of Labor Statistics
Current Employment Statistics Survey

(BLS Household Survey indicates a smaller but still substantial employment shortfall.)

Why was aggregate demand inadequate? Monetary policy could not be seriously faulted. The Federal Reserve eased money so much that real federal funds rates remained near zero for a considerable period. As we shall see, improperly designed fiscal stimulus failed to correct the inadequate demand. But first we must dispose of another possible cause, inflation due to weak structural competition.

Sometimes monetary and fiscal stimulus must be held down due to the failure of *structural* competition to hold inflation in check. But that was not the case in this recessionary period. Structural competition (the intensity of competition built into product, service, labor, and financial markets) is the *controller* that channels demand into increased production rather than into increased prices. Structural competition is intensified by factors such as international trade, effective antitrust laws, and opportunities for potential competitors to acquire capital and education necessary to enter markets. It is impeded by factors such as cost-enhancing government regulations, aggressive labor unions, and international cartels such as OPEC. For the first time in more than thirty years, the intensity of competition built into the structure of the economy had been strong enough for a considerable period to hold the core inflation rate within an acceptable zone. We did not have to hold down demand stimulus to prevent inflation.

Inadequate aggregate demand was due to the faulty design of fiscal policy. For decades fiscal policy had been shunned as a tool to stimulate demand because of its inflexibility. Fiscal policy is ordinarily changed only once a year, in the annual budget, which usually takes six months or longer to be enacted. The fiscal stimulus packages of 2001–3 showed no improvement in flexibility. They could not be changed easily when found to be inadequate to bring quick recovery. (Imagine how ineffective monetary policy would be in controlling inflation if the Federal Reserve could change course only once a year.) We must adopt a flexible fiscal stimulus plan.

One Plan to Provide Flexible Fiscal Stimulus

The extreme difficulty of predicting the needed amount of fiscal stimulus more than two or three months in advance dictates the requirements of an effective stimulative fiscal policy:

• The program must be flexible—quick to start and easy to stop when fiscal stimulus is no longer necessary. Also, it needs the ability to make midcourse corrections.

• The program should not involve overhauling the tax code or initiating long-term spending programs. Bad long-term law, hastily designed, can too easily be passed under the pressure to provide quick, short-term stimulation. Long-term tax and spending bills should pass or fail on their own merits, not because a temporary stimulus to the economy is needed.

• Legislative authorization must be set up in advance to facilitate a quick start.

Following is one plan that meets the above requirements. Congress should provide permanent authorization for the president to have "Social Security tax rebate" checks averaging, say, $100 to $500, mailed every three months to anyone who has paid Social Security taxes anytime in the previous three years. The average amount of each mailing would depend on the expected need for fiscal stimulation for the coming three months. Actual amounts mailed to each individual would be proportional to the amount of Social Security taxes paid by the worker over the previous three years. Most of the unemployed would receive checks. These payments would not weaken the incentive to work. Only those currently working or having recently worked would receive checks. The rebates can be called "retroactive, temporary tax cuts."

Of course, we cannot raid the Social Security trust fund just to gain temporary fiscal stimulation, so payment would come from general Treasury funds. The Social Security system would be involved only to the extent of providing mailing lists. The secretary of the Treasury would maintain constant consultation with the Federal Reserve and with the president's economic advisers to determine when fiscal stimulus was needed and the amount of the quarterly payment.

If Congress unwisely insisted on making each quarterly decision as to the need for, and the amount of, the stimulating payment, automatic mechanisms would have to be devised to bring the decision to a vote quickly and to keep extraneous matters from being considered.

The plan would give the president (or Congress) a flexibility in stimulating the economy almost equal to that of the Federal Reserve in controlling inflation. The plan has built-in controls against abuse. Overstimulation that threatened inflation would call forth a rebuke by the Federal Reserve in the form of tight money with unpopular rising interest rates. The president (or Congress) would also be anxious to end the program to allow funding for permanent spending and tax-cutting proposals.

This policy would make future recessions even shorter and milder than the little ones we have experienced in the last twenty years. Furthermore, it would lift from the Federal Reserve the necessity of making highly aggressive interest rate cuts such as those made in 2002 and 2003. Extremely low short-term rates work a hardship on the millions of people who rely on interest from savings accounts and other short-term investments, slowing their spending in the process. Also, very low interest rates sometimes create a bubble in the housing market, adding serious instability to the economy. That may have happened in the 2000–2004 period, especially in a number of large cities. The destabilizing impact of very low interest rates on the future economy should not be underestimated.

The Plan as a Tool for Managing Expectations

Government management of expectations is of critical importance in maintaining strong economic growth. Managing expectations has already proven its worth in controlling inflation. A simple declaration by the Federal Reserve that it will maintain price stability has gone a long way toward achieving that goal. A business manager knows that he will be living in an environment of moderate increases in wages and prices, and to remain competitive he must manage his cost structure accordingly. He must avoid excessive wage increases. Expectations of limited inflation have done much to make reasonable price stability possible.

The flexible fiscal stimulus plan does the same thing for insuring adequate aggregate demand. Once adopted, the plan tells consumers and managers that government support of aggregate demand by tax rebates will be continued in times of recession (although in diminishing amounts) *until full employment is approached or the threat of inflation becomes apparent*. Such expectations will encourage consumers to spend and business managers to invest in new capacity and technical upgrades while holding costs and prices in line.

With a flexible fiscal stimulus policy added to the Federal Reserve inflation control policy already in place, we will have far better tools to manage aggregate demand than this country has ever had before. The prospect of stable growth in demand should be improved. Then we can turn to the critically important problem of maintaining structural competition sufficiently intense to channel aggregate demand into production rather than into price increases. This problem will be examined in Chapters 3 and 4.

Likely Effects of the Plan on Federal Deficits

Worry about increasing the deficit will most likely prompt objections to this flexible fiscal stimulus plan. *Actually, deficits under the plan would likely be smaller than without the plan.* It is highly probable that fiscal stimulus begun early and used aggressively would keep the (taxable) spending-income-spending stream growing fast enough so that deficits over a much smaller recession (even with the mailing of stimulative checks) would actually be less than would occur over the life of the longer recession that would otherwise prevail. Even aggressive mailing of Social Security tax rebates *averaging* \$500 a quarter for several quarters beginning in early 2001 (amounting to about \$70 billion each quarter) would likely have added less to the deficit than losing almost one trillion dollars in tax revenue in 2001 to 2004 that the federal government *would have received* had the economy recovered quickly to the full-employment level. This lost revenue was due to the slowing economy, not the cuts in tax rates. Some analysts have estimated that a third of the 2001–4 federal deficit was due to the tax cuts. This is probably not true. The deficit would have been even higher without the tax cuts because the (taxable) spending-income stream would have grown much more slowly, reducing federal receipts even more. Furthermore, three or four more years will be required to return to full employment. Much more tax revenue will be lost.

The tax cuts in 2001 and 2003 were both followed by temporary surges in real personal consumption expenditures. Since consumer spending accounts for about two-thirds of all spending, these two surges in spending by consumers had a significant effect in supporting total spending (and, of course, output and employment) in the economy. Without those two surges in consumer spending, spending by business would have been lower, the recession would have been much deeper, and the recovery would have been slower. The (taxable) spending-income stream would have been smaller and the deficit larger.

Tax rebates have a *multiplied* impact on the (taxable) spending-income stream as measured by nominal GDP. They increase consumer spending, which generates more income, which generates more spending, and so on. Furthermore, the increase in consumer spending stimulates business spending for plant, equipment, and inventories.

As shown in Chart 1.2, federal tax receipts fluctuate along with (but more widely than) the taxable spending-income stream measured by nominal GDP. So tax rebates would push up tax receipts considerably faster than they push up nominal GDP. The deficit would shrink.

Chart 1.2 Annual Percentage Change in Nominal GDP and Tax Receipts

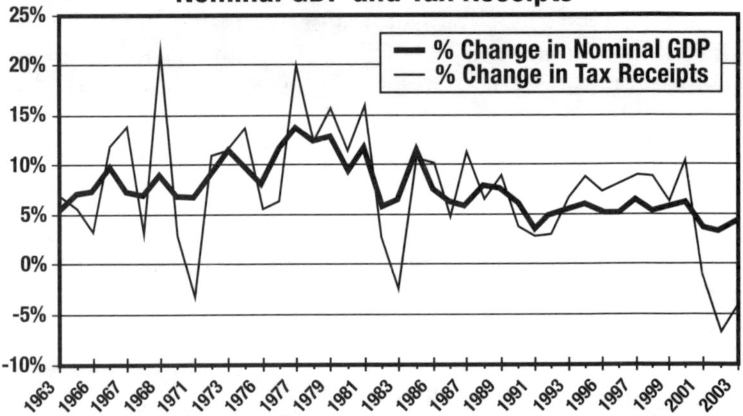

Source: Congressional Budget Office

Benefits from the flexible fiscal stimulus plan would be great enough to warrant its adoption even if it increased the deficit. The likelihood that the plan would actually reduce the deficit that would otherwise prevail makes its attractiveness overwhelming.

Do Deficits Matter?

Deficits matter. Why? Because they add to the national

debt. Does the national debt matter? Yes, it does. Why? Because it requires that taxes be levied each year on someone to raise the funds to pay the interest on the debt. Taxes are unpleasant. Any tax levied to pay interest on the debt makes more difficult the raising of tax money for essential government services.

In two opposite situations, efforts should be made to reduce any existing deficit. A deficit means the government is adding to total spending by pouring more money into the spending-income stream than it is taking out. In times of inflation, additions to the spending-income stream aggravate that inflation. Faster inflation requires greater Federal Reserve restraint in the form of higher interest rates and thus impedes capital spending by business. This is the well-known "crowding out" of investment by government deficit financing. In this situation the deficit should be reduced by cutting government spending or increasing taxes.

In times of *recession or slow growth*, efforts should also be made to eliminate the deficit. But this can only be done by increasing the (taxable) spending-income stream that generates increased revenue. And that can only be done by *reducing* taxes or *increasing* spending, the opposite to the remedy in inflationary times. (This assumes monetary stimulation has been used to the fullest extent feasible.) Such action *must* be taken with a flexible program so that it can be slowed and stopped once business activity recovers.

Few economists would argue that we can eliminate a deficit *in times of recession or slow growth due to inadequate demand* by raising taxes or cutting spending. That would reduce the (taxable) spending-income stream and *increase* the deficit. Shouldn't the opposite approach increase the (taxable) spending-income stream and *reduce* the deficit?

In between these two extremes, economic conditions may require a certain amount of government deficit financing. The long-term need for continuing deficits to support aggregate demand, if they are needed at all, will depend on a number of unpredictable factors such as the saving rate, international capital flows, and the capital-output ratio.

As this is written in the fall of 2004, many articles are appearing warning quite properly that action must be taken to reduce the huge federal deficits projected for several years under present tax and spending policies. Those same articles point out that no realistic proposals to reduce the deficit are coming from any part of the political establishment. The outlook appears grim. That outlook will change.

As we approach full employment, large deficits will raise the threat of *imminent* inflation. That will raise alarms in bond and stock markets and at the Federal Reserve. Those alarms will concentrate the minds of the president and of legislators fearful of crashing bond and stock prices and a subsequent recession. Spending cuts and/or tax increases will follow, and the deficit will be brought under control. It may not happen smoothly, but it will happen.

The Plan and the Inflation Problem

Many people will argue that government borrowing to pay out stimulative tax rebates would aggravate inflation. That is not likely when substantial inflation-restraining *below-capacity* competition exists in periods of recession and slow growth. (Below-capacity competition is the increased intensity of competition that exists when output drops farther below full capacity. Firms compete more aggressively for orders, and workers compete more aggressively for jobs, as will be described in Chapter 3.) But if the economy is suffering from weak competition built into the structure of the economy, and inflation is a problem, stimulative tax rebates should be used only sparingly if at all. Efforts should be directed toward eliminating the impediments to inflation-controlling structural competition. But that is a slow process, and a country may have to suffer through a period of unsatisfactory high unemployment while those impediments are removed, as has been the case in parts of Europe over the past several years.

Structural competition was weak in the United States for the entire period from 1965 to about the mid-1990s. Excessive inflation was nearly always a problem. During that period many economists argued that stimulation of the economy could not bring unemployment down below 6 percent without triggering inflation. Six percent was considered to be the lowest possible non-accelerating-inflation rate of unemployment (NAIRU). This was true during the long period when structural competition was weak, but it is not true at this time. Nevertheless, as we shall see in Chapter 4, unwise government policies adopted under pressure to increase social services could raise impediments to effective structural competition and revive the problem of inflation due to that weakening competition.

Appraising the 2001 and 2003 Stimulative Tax Cuts

The tax cuts of 2001 and 2003 were passed to provide an immediate demand-side stimulus to the economy and to improve incentives to work, save, and invest by cutting marginal income tax rates, taxes on capital gains, and taxes on dividends. The following observations can be made about the tax cuts:

• Without the tax cuts, the recession would have been deeper.

• The tax cuts had the virtue of reintroducing the use of fiscal stimulus to spur the economy as monetary stimulus proved inadequate.

• The tax-cut plans also had the virtue of reintroducing tax rebates as a device to get spendable money into the hands of consumers without breaking the ties between work and income. (They had been used just slightly by the Ford administration.)

• The tax-cut plans could not make midcourse corrections as they proved inadequate to bring full recovery quickly. No one is wise enough to predict how much fiscal stimulus will be needed. That's why a flexible plan is needed.

• The tax cuts were revisions in the tax code with long-lasting impacts, passed in large part for temporary stimulation. Long-term modifications of the tax code and long-term spending programs should pass or fail on their own merits, not because of the need for short-term stimulus.

• A *permanent* tax-cut stimulus cannot usually be designed that will provide adequate short-term stimulus without overstimulating the economy in later years. The 2001 tax cut was certainly inadequate to bring quick recovery, yet it raised great concern about overstimulus in later years.

• Justification for the tax cuts was of a peculiar nature. They were justified largely as necessary to improve incentives to invest by reducing marginal income tax rates, taxes on capital gains, and taxes on dividends. This was in spite of the fact that the existing tax rates had in the last half of the 1990s produced *excessive* stock market investment, *excessive* plant and equipment investment, and *excessive* venture capital investment. Were incentives better than those that had produced excessive investment in the previous years really necessary? More about this in Chapter 5.

Summary of the Case for Flexible Fiscal Stimulus

We have learned from painful experience that we must stop *inflation* early before trends are well established. We must now learn to stop *recessions* early. The only way that can be done is by a flexible fiscal stimulus plan put in place before the beginning of an economic downturn.

In the future, declines in business activity requiring fiscal stimulus will certainly appear again in spite of aggressive, stabilizing monetary policy. The pressure to maintain full employment is so strong that fiscal stimulus *will* be used. If no flexible plan is in place, fiscal stimulus will likely be used badly.

Excessive monetary ease can be counterproductive by driving interest rates too low, working hardships on those relying on savings incomes, and by adding later instability to bond and home prices. Use of flexible fiscal stimulus will make extreme monetary ease unnecessary.

If structural competition is weak as evidenced by above-target inflation coexistent with above-target unemployment (as it was for most of the 1965–95 period), supplementary fiscal stimulation should be used sparingly or not at all. Efforts should be directed toward reducing impediments to structural competition.

The use of flexible fiscal stimulation will reduce the danger of the enactment of long-term spending or tax proposals under the guise of the need for temporary stimulation. Long-term initiatives should stand or fall on their own long-term merits, not as a temporary stimulating device.

Reducing employment shortfalls similar to the 2001–4 experience is essential both to reduce human distress and to reduce pressure to slow (or reverse) the expansion of free international trade. Those protectionist efforts always blossom in periods of high unemployment.

An improvement in our ability to manage aggregate demand has been one of the most important forces behind our improving economic performance over the past half century. The adoption of a flexible fiscal stimulus plan is the single most important gap yet to be filled.

The Immediate Employment Problem

Government faces the problem of creating about ten million jobs to absorb the growth in the labor force and to return to full employment in the next four or five years. It can be done. But great effort will be required to avoid two dangers: inadequate demand and inflation due to weakened structural competition.

As for the demand danger, the economy turned sluggish again in June 2004, and as of this writing in the fall of that year has gained only moderate traction. If the economy weakens again in 2005, further fiscal stimulation will be needed immediately, and a flexible fiscal stimulus plan should be enacted promptly to provide that stimulus unless, of course, inflation accelerates sharply.

A special danger to the adequacy of demand lies in the coming end to the surge in home prices that prevailed in several cities in the past few years. The increase in home prices was without doubt important in sustaining consumer demand. Hundreds of billions of dollars in cash were taken out of home equity by refinancing, by home equity loans, and by selling one home and keeping part of the funds when buying a new home. That cash added substantially to consumer spending. The wealth effect from rising home prices also added to consumer spending. Increases in home prices will slow from their recent surge. When home price increases slow, or home prices perhaps even decline, they will reduce an important support for consumer spending. Government will not likely be able to predict the timing or depth of such a possible weakening of consumer spending. A *flexible* fiscal stimulus plan is needed to keep demand growing smoothly. If consumer spending slows appreciably, the Federal Reserve will not be able to stimulate demand enough to offset that weakening quickly enough. The Federal Reserve cannot cut interest rates much below the current low level.

Needless to say, several other surprise events may be waiting in the wings to slow aggregate demand. We wonder how any administration could dare forego a flexible fiscal stimulus plan that would provide a powerful tool to maintain aggregate demand.

The danger of inflation arising from the weakening of structural competition is a far more insidious danger. Political pressures are mounting to improve social services including Social Security, Medicare, and environmental protection. If not carefully designed, an expansion in social services will raise compliance costs to business and thereby erect impediments to the ability of structural competition to control inflation. As Chapter 3 will indicate, social service programs have aggravated inflation before. No fiscal stimulus plan can overcome that obstacle. Chapter 4 describes the current inflation danger from increased compliance costs in considerable detail.

Many possible potholes may become evident on the road to full employment. A flexible fiscal stimulus plan can circumnavigate some of them.

Our Debt to the Less Talented

We must add another section to this chapter to point out that we owe a heavy debt to the less talented (and to other low-paid workers) among us. That debt can be reduced a little bit by a flexible fiscal stimulus plan that will reduce unemployment. What is that debt?

As will be argued in Chapter 3, much of our prosperity is due to increased international trade and competition. That trade and competition, along with extensive immigration, have put heavy downward pressure on the wages of low-paid, less-talented workers, more so than on the incomes of any other group. And so the less talented pay an excessive price for the international trade that is so beneficial to us all.

High unemployment hurts low-wage workers most of all, compounding the pain they bear for the benefits we all enjoy from international trade. We have a special duty to the less talented to prevent periods of employment shortfall such as we have experienced in 2001–4. We must maintain full employment so that a worker laid off due to foreign competition can have a better chance of finding another job quickly in another line of work.

To be born with a genetic heritage that provides few talents, and to grow up in a family that fails to nurture even those few inherited talents, is a heavy burden to carry. That burden is compounded when a government unnecessarily allows extensive unemployment to persist. Unemployment is especially hard on the less talented. It can be ameliorated somewhat by a flexible fiscal stimulus plan.

The Retirement Problem

Those workers born between 1943 and 1959 will have a full retirement age of 66, and those born in 1960 and later will have a full retirement age of 67. Even that extension of the retirement age may not be enough to compensate for the expanding life span and declining birthrate. There may not be enough working people to support the growing ranks of the elderly. Somehow a larger proportion of the elderly will have to be enticed back into the labor force. That will be harder to do if unemployment is not held at a very low level.

In Conclusion

We have few problems that are not made more difficult by extensive unemployment. A flexible fiscal stimulus plan is not a luxury. It is a necessity. We can learn better how to manage aggregate demand. The New Economy can evolve to a higher employment performance. To repeat, we cannot let past performance set standards for the future. We can learn. We can and will do better.

Chapter 2

TAMING STOCK MARKET BUBBLES

Stock market bubbles add instability to a market economy. While forming, they add unsustainable demand to the system. That demand is sometimes inflationary. When they burst, they make more difficult the sustaining of sufficient aggregate demand to maintain full employment. We have the evidence in the United States of 2001 through 2004. In Japan, more than a decade of stagnation followed the far greater 1980s bubble in both stocks and real estate. Mini-bubbles will always be with us, but bubbles of the late 1990s variety can at least be attenuated by appropriate Federal Reserve action. Bubble control would be another important step in improving the management of aggregate demand.

The Congressional Mandate

In 1934 the Congress, smarting from the human devastation caused by the Great Depression, gave the responsibility for controlling excessive use of stock market credit to the Board of Governors of the Federal Reserve System. Excessive speculation in the late 1920s, financed by credit, was believed to have been a significant cause of the Depression. The Securities and Exchange Act stated: "For the purpose of preventing the excessive use of credit for the purchase or carrying of securities, the Board of Governors of the Federal Reserve System *shall*, prior to October 1, 1934, and from time to time thereafter, *prescribe rules and regulations* with respect to the amount of credit that may be initially extended and subsequently maintained on any security . . . " (italics ours).

This mandate was softened only to the extent of allowing the Board to use its judgment in prescribing rules and regulations. The Congress did not soften the *responsibility* it had given to the Board to prevent the excessive use of credit for purchasing or holding securities.

How should the Federal Reserve exercise this mandate? It has two basic tools: general credit controls that suppress the entire economy and the authority to set margin requirements that limit the amount of credit that can be used for purchasing and carrying stocks. It also has a third, less formal, tool—intimidation. The use of this tool will be described later in the chapter. When stock speculation produces a bubble at a *time of general price inflation*, the Federal Reserve should tighten credit, thereby slowing the entire economy until inflation subsides. In limiting general inflation the Federal Reserve will also subdue stock speculation. In addition to tightening general credit controls, raising margin requirements might help dampen inflationary expectations and reduce somewhat the need for the general tightening of the broad credit controls.

But the big problem arises when stock speculation is rampant at a time when prices are stable. The tightening of general credit controls that slow the entire economy seems like a blunt instrument to be used to curb stock speculation at a time when the economy doesn't need to be slowed. In such cases, raising margin requirements should at least be tried to curb speculation without depressing the entire economy and increasing unemployment.

The Federal Reserve and the 1996–2000 Stock Market Bubble

Only twice in the past half century has stock speculation been rampant when the general price level was stable. The 1996–2000 period was one of those times. The Federal Reserve did not use any of its tools to curb speculation until late 1999 when it slightly tapped the interest rate brake.

We read the minutes and transcripts of the meetings of the Open Market Committee and the directives issued by the Committee for the entire period in which the bubble formed. Some Committee members frequently referred to increasing, dangerous speculation that was forming a bubble, implying that a dangerous collapse was possible. They frequently mentioned that stock price movements have important impacts on the overall economy. They were clearly aware of the dangers of the bubble. And yet there was not a single statement acknowledging the *responsibility* the Congress had given the Federal Reserve to prevent the excessive use of credit for the purchase or carrying of securities. (The Federal Reserve had tried twice to get the Congress to remove that responsibility—in 1985 and 1995. Each time the Congress refused.) Furthermore, the Committee apparently never discussed the possibility of the Federal Reserve increasing margin requirements to slow bubble expansion. These were the specific tools given to the Federal Reserve to be used to restrain excessive use of credit.

Apparently the Federal Reserve did not raise margin requirements to dampen the late 1990s bubble because the Board of Governors did not believe margin requirements could effectively limit speculation. The reason usually given is that stocks held on credit amount to less than 2 percent of the total value of outstanding stocks. Therefore prices (and speculation) could proceed independently of margin limitations. This view was not always held. Verbatim transcripts of the September 24, 1996 meeting include a statement by Chairman Greenspan, commenting about the problem of dampening a stock market bubble. He said, "We do have the possibility of raising major concerns by increasing margin requirements. I guarantee that if you want to get rid of the bubble, whatever it is, that will do it. My concern is that I am not sure what else it will do." The use of margin requirements was apparently mentioned in Open Market Committee meetings only one other time and *was never discussed.*[1]

Use of Margin Requirements From World War II to 1974

Since the Securities Exchange Act was passed in 1934, the Federal Reserve has changed margin requirements twenty-two times, eighteen of those times from the end of World War II to 1974, *after which they left requirements unchanged at 50 percent.* Chart 2.1 shows those changes together with margin loans outstanding and S&P 500 stock prices. Note that only once did the Federal Reserve use margin requirements aggressively, in 1945–46, raising them in three steps to 100 percent. This was done against a background of stock speculation and upward pressure on consumer prices as wartime wage and price control deteriorated. That was the only time that the Federal Reserve *by their actions* said to the

Chart 2.1 S&P 500 and Margin Loans

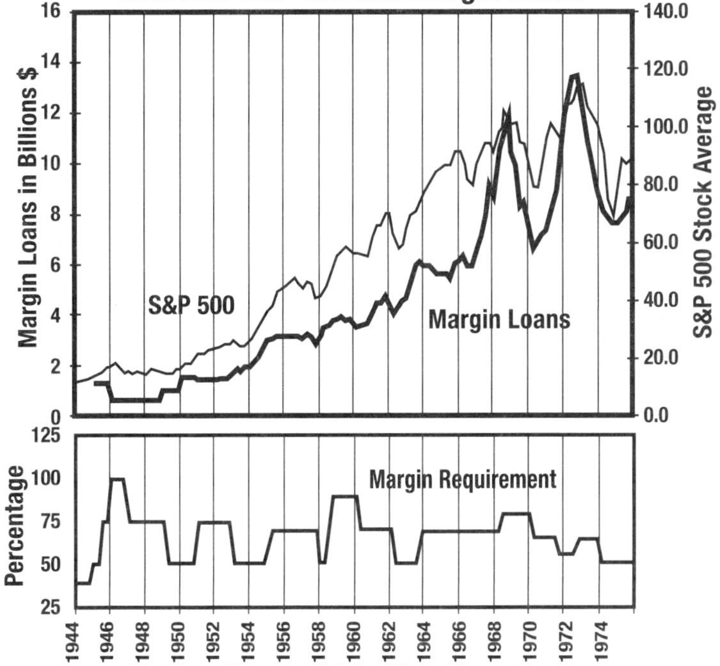

Sources: "Banking and Monetary Statistics," Federal Reserve Board; Federal Reserve Flow of Funds Table

markets, "We believe speculation is dangerously excessive."

As the Federal Reserve raised margin requirements in 1945, margin credit began to decline. Stock prices began to level off after the increase in requirements to 100 percent in January 1946. They peaked in May 1946 and dropped sharply beginning in August, but only after the Federal Reserve raised the discount rate. Raising margin requirements in 1945 must be considered a success in reducing the use of credit for speculative purposes, and at least a partial success in limiting speculation and stock price increases in general.

A careful examination of the chart indicates that the next four *moderate* increases (1951, 1955, 1958, and 1963) in margin requirements apparently stopped the growth of margin credit, but what was the impact on stock prices? *In no case did speculation continue sufficiently to produce a subsequent decline of even 25 percent in the S&P 500 monthly stock prices.* (A 40-percent decline in stock prices is sometimes used as a benchmark to call the previous speculation a bubble.) Importantly, the two subsequent *major* bursts of margin credit in 1967–68 and 1971–72 that accompanied sharply rising stock prices were *not* met by significant attempts by the Federal Reserve to restrain the use of stock-market credit, and the meager restraint that the Federal Reserve did provide came very late. Both of these speculative episodes were followed by serious declines in stock prices. The first decline was 29 percent. The second was 43 percent. Both episodes coincided with Federal Reserve failure to rein in rapidly worsening general inflation. Had the Federal Reserve tightened money sufficiently to stabilize the general price level, stock speculation would surely have been curtailed even without an increase in margin requirements.

In summary, then, during this thirty-year period in which the Federal Reserve *toyed* with margin requirements as a tool to control credit-financed speculation, only once (1945–46) were margin requirements raised aggressively. They appear to have been effective. In the next four episodes of moderate credit expansion the Federal Reserve became much less aggressive in using those controls, but even these efforts were moderately successful. Finally, in the two important bouts of credit expansion in 1967–68 and 1971–72 margin requirement increases were just tiny baby steps and came very late. *We cannot say from this experience that margin controls will be ineffective when properly used. They simply have not yet been adequately tested.*

Nonuse of Margin Controls From 1974 to the Present

In 1974 the Federal Reserve quit using margin requirements to dampen speculation. In the thirty years since 1974 there have been two times when margin controls should probably have been used—in 1986–87 and in the late 1990s. The 1986–87 episode of speculation ended with the crash of September 1987, a quick decline of 27 percent in the S&P 500. The late 1990s episode ended with the bear market of 2000–2003, a decline of 43 percent in the S&P 500. These two periods were marked by frothy speculation and a rapid rise in stock market credit, both of which the Congress had given the Federal Reserve the responsibility to control. But also, both of these periods witnessed reasonably stable general prices, making undesirable the use of general credit control to slow the economy.

How should the Federal Reserve have faced this problem? *With the benefit of hindsight* we suggest the following. The Federal Reserve should have increased margin requirements in several speculation-unnerving steps to 100 percent. If this failed to curb speculation, the Federal Reserve should have turned to their third, less formal tool—*intimidation*. By repeating, frequently and publicly, the worries about the bubble that were expressed by some governors in the Open Market Committee meetings, the Federal Reserve would have raised fear that they would use general credit controls to dampen speculation. By doing so they would have sharply increased the *risk* of speculative stock commitments. This would likely have dampened speculation. It would have helped to offset the absurd forecasts coming from many members of the financial community caught up in the New Economy frenzy. Perhaps these steps, accompanied by a slight tap on the interest-rate brake, would have dampened the bubble significantly.

Why Did the Federal Reserve Abandon the Use of Margin Requirements?

We have already cited the reason given by the Federal Reserve: the governors didn't believe that changing margin requirements would be effective. As we have seen, the record does not entirely support that conviction. But there are more fundamental reasons why the use of margin requirements was abandoned.

Robert J. Shiller, professor of economics at Yale's International Center for Finance, has made a cogent observation that resonates with us about the reason that the Federal Reserve after 1974 abandoned the use of margin requirements to dampen stock market speculation. He suggests that that decision coincided with the arrival of the "efficient market" theory of stock pricing. That theory contends that the market always reflects everything that can be *known* about a stock or the market in general. Therefore, the market is always right as far as can be *known*.[2] We suggest that this is not true. The market does not reflect everything that can be *known* about a stock or the market in general. Rather it often reflects rabid *emotions* along with some *knowledge*. Consequently, the market is not always right.

The efficient market doctrine took much of the country by storm, and, as Professor Shiller suggests, may have been partly responsible for the Federal Reserve abandoning its previous efforts (tentative though they had been) to restrain excessive stock speculation financed by credit. Why try to interfere with a market that is always right? The efficient market theory appears to be fading away. It is another bad idea whose disappearance will add to the quality of accumulated knowledge.

THE DIFFICULTY OF IDENTIFYING BUBBLES

Still another—even more fundamental—reason lies behind the Federal Reserve decision not to attempt to prevent excessive stock market speculation. It is the extreme difficulty of identifying bubbles.

To control bubbles the Federal Reserve cannot just raise margin requirements to restrain speculative froth and sharp rises in margin credit and then back off when these two features quiet down. The Japanese did that for a dozen years, during which stock prices on the Tokyo stock exchange rose about eight times in one of the great stock market bubbles of all times. Each time speculative froth appeared, margin requirements were raised moderately and remained there until speculation quieted down. After margin requirements were reduced, stock prices began to rise again, and the bubble grew.

To prevent a bubble, a central bank would have to restrain credit not just until the speculation quieted down but as long as prices remained high or perhaps even until prices declined. And that requires an estimation of the intrinsic value of stocks that is difficult to make. The intrinsic value of stocks depends on difficult-to-predict future events about which stockholders strongly disagree.

If Federal Reserve governors are to use margin requirements or any other tool to prevent bubbles, they must be prepared to tell the world that they think stock prices are too high at a time when many stockholders believe otherwise and are very much interested in seeing them go higher. Those stockholders will be loud in their criticism. That fact would likely prevent the overuse of margin controls.

No one can fault the Federal Reserve for wishing to shed the responsibility of restraining undue speculation. It is a difficult and thankless job. But the Federal Reserve is the only organization that can do it. If it doesn't, we must live with the occasional bubble and its adverse consequences.

Housing Price Bubbles

We have said nothing in this chapter about containing bubbles in home prices. If they occur in inflationary times, they should be contained by general credit restraint that slows the economy. But general credit controls are not practical if the bubble develops in a period such as 2001–4 when demand is insufficient to achieve full employment and *inflation is not a problem.* A flexible fiscal stimulus plan as described in Chapter 1 would obviate the need for extreme monetary easing as has prevailed in the recent period and thus would likely prevent a real estate bubble from forming.

In Conclusion

This entire chapter may be unnecessary. The painful

aftermath of the 1990s bubble may remain strong enough in memory to prevent another bubble from developing for many years. Nevertheless, we believe that the failure to use margin requirement restraint in the 1990s was a mistake. Margin requirement restraint is a useful, though unpopular, tool. It should be kept, polished and ready, available for use in the next bout of irrational exuberance. Who knows when animal spirits will light the flames of speculation again.

Chapter 3

ACHIEVING 4 PERCENT UNEMPLOYMENT

The goal of a low average 4 percent unemployment rate is finally within reach. This chapter describes the historic developments leading up to the present opportunity. It also outlines the policies necessary to complete that evolution. Average unemployment over 4 percent for two or three years should henceforth be considered a mistake of government management of the economic environment by concurrent or previous administrations.

THE TWO ESSENTIALS

As described in Chapter 1, two basic conditions are necessary to maintain a full-employment economy coexistent with low inflation: *adequate (but not excessive) aggregate demand and intense structural competition.*

First, the spending of money by individuals, businesses, and governments (demand in the marketplace) is the necessary *initiator* of economic activity. It activates the placing of orders, the hiring of workers, and the paying out of income. Without adequate spending, nothing much gets done. We have recessions and periods of slow growth. Second, structural competition (the intensity of competition built into product, service, labor, and financial markets) is the *controller* that channels demand into increased production rather than into increased prices. Structural competition is intensified by factors such as international trade, effective antitrust laws, and opportunities for potential competitors to acquire capital and education necessary to enter markets. It is impeded by factors such as cost-enhancing government regulations, aggressive labor unions, and international cartels such as OPEC.

If structural competition is not sufficiently intense to hold inflation within an acceptable zone as demand increases, the Federal Reserve has to reduce demand by tightening money to slow the economy below full-capacity operating rates. That action increases competition sufficiently to restrain inflation. At lower operating rates, firms compete more aggressively for scarce orders, and workers compete more aggressively for limited job openings. The increased competition due to slower rates of output can be called *below-capacity competition.* The weaker the intensity of structural competition, the more below-capacity competition is required to restrain price increases. Below-capacity competition shows up as unemployment in the labor market.

Every recession since World War II has been preceded by (precipitated by?) Federal Reserve tightening of money. And every such episode of Federal Reserve restraint has been induced by a failure of structural competition to hold the inflation rate within an acceptable zone. *Inflation must be controlled by competition in a market-managed economy. If not by structural competition, it will be controlled by below-capacity competition with its increased unemployment.*

The intensity of structural competition is determined by factors on the supply side of markets. This is the important realm of microeconomics. Following is a list of factors, both positive and negative, that we or others have cited as affecting the supply side of market performance.

Positive factors:

- International trade
- Effective antitrust enforcement
- Improved sources of financing, especially for entrepreneurs
- Improved access to education

Negative factors:

- High marginal tax rates that reduce incentives to work, save, and invest
- Government regulations that increase compliance costs
- Oil shocks induced by the OPEC oil cartel
- High welfare payments that discourage work

Each of these supply-side factors has an impact on structural competition. That is, they impact the ability of the market to direct aggregate demand into efficient production rather than into price increases. In making forecasts, the best way to arrive at the total impact of changes in all these supply-side factors is to estimate their total impact on inflation. Controlling inflation is the primary (but not the only) function of structural competition.

Chart 3.1 shows the *inverse* relationship between inflation and the productivity growth rate (much more about this in Chapter 6). While intense structural competition is limiting inflation, it is also enhancing productivity. And in limiting inflation, it is also limiting the need for below-capacity competition with its unpleasant unemployment. Thus intense structural competition creates New Economy conditions: rapidly growing productivity and low unemployment coexistent with low inflation. The sum of the inflationary impacts of all supply-side factors (positive and negative) can be identified as a measure of the intensity of structural competition. Therefore in this book we use the terms *supply side and structural competition* almost interchangeably.

Chart 3.1 Changes in the CPI and Business Productivity, Three-Year Moving Average

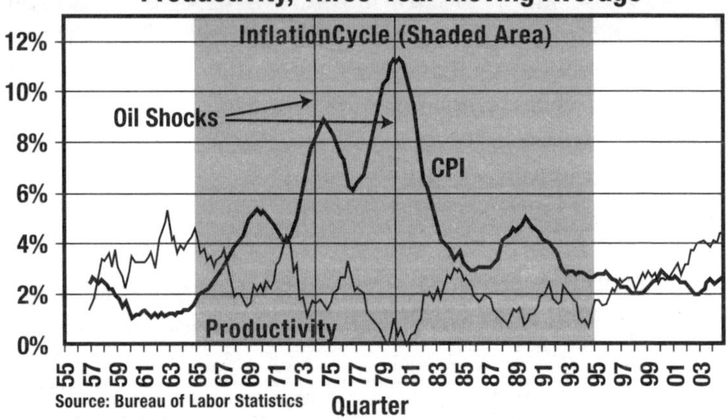

The intensity of structural competition is not a constant. It often exhibits moderate changes from year to year and sometimes has large, long-lasting swings. The thirty-year inflation cycle (shown on Chart 3.1) that began in 1965, peaked in 1980, and then took almost fifteen years to heal was one of the defining episodes of the twentieth century. As will be described later in this chapter, factors that reduced the intensity of structural competition in the late 1960s and early 1970s were major causes of that inflation cycle.

The intensity of *structural* competition together with the intensity of *below-capacity* competition make up the intensity of *overall* competition. The inflation rate is a reasonable *inverse* measure of the intensity of overall competition. When overall competition weakens, the inflation rate accelerates. The intensity of *overall* competition weakened from 1965 to 1980, allowing the inflation rate to rise substantially as Chart 3.1 shows. But during that period *below-capacity* competition as measured by the unemployment rate and the capacity utilization rate *strengthened* substantially. If overall competition weakened and below-capacity competition strengthened, then *structural* competition (the other part of overall competition) must have weakened dramatically. After 1980 overall competition strengthened, as evidenced by the slowing inflation rate. Below-capacity competition weakened as we approached full employment. Therefore structural competition (the other part of overall competition) must have strengthened dramatically.

What does this mean for the coming years? The Federal Reserve has quite properly resolved to maintain price stability. Most central banks are targeting an inflation rate of about 2 to 3 percent. The Federal Reserve will likely conform to that range. That means that *overall* competition must be maintained at a relatively stable intensity to preserve that price stability. If *structural* competition should weaken, inflation will accelerate, and the Federal Reserve will be required to supplement that competition with greater *below-capacity* competition. The economy will slow, and unemployment will rise. In the following chapter we describe how political pressures are building to improve social services including Social Security, Medicare, and environmental protection. If actions are taken that increase compliance costs to business, they will impede the ability of structural competition to restrain prices. Inflation will accelerate. Accelerating inflation will be followed by Federal Reserve restraint to increase below-capacity competition to supplement the weakening structural competition. That means higher unemployment. In Chapter 4 we describe ways by which some of these political pressures can be met without inflation and unemployment.

Need for Government Management of the Market Environment

Neither adequate demand nor sufficiently intense structural competition occurs automatically. Both must be managed by government (including the central bank). It was once believed that aggregate demand required no management. Supply, it was argued, automatically creates sufficient effective demand to purchase all goods being produced. But that bad idea is gone forever.

As for structural competition, government has two responsibilities. It must maintain adequate competition by such positive moves as antitrust prevention of monopolistic practices. But just as important, it must refrain from erecting impediments to competition by regulation or other actions that increase compliance costs and limit the ability of competition to hold prices down.

No matter how much we wish it were not so, the success of the economy depends heavily on the ability of government to maintain intense structural competition and adequate but not excessive aggregate demand in the marketplace.

A forecaster's success will depend largely on the ability to forecast government's success or failure in managing those two factors. For example, during and following the 2001 recession some forecasters were predicting an *extended* period of below 2 percent growth in the United States. Included in this forecast were *implicit* predictions that unemployment would rise above 10 percent and that government would be unwilling or unable to prevent that move. Those implicit predictions do not seem plausible.

In forecasting it is as important to predict government responses (and the success thereof) to an event as *it is to predict the event itself.* It is positively amazing to read forecasts of coming dire events with no mention of how government will respond and how successful those responses might be. In forecasting the evolution of the New Economy we are really appraising the possible success of government to manage structural competition and aggregate demand.

Some conservatives lay the blame for most of our economic troubles on government intervention in economic activity. They argue that the economy would work just fine if government would just get out of the way. They may be distressed to read that successful economic performance depends on government management of aggregate demand and structural competition. Actually they should be delighted.

If government (including the Federal Reserve) properly manages aggregate demand and maintains adequate structural competition, the need for government management of the minutia of market activity declines. When government fails to maintain adequate demand to keep the economy growing near full employment or fails to maintain structural competition sufficiently intense to channel that demand into production rather than inflation, pressure always grows to protect workers from foreign competition, aid declining industries, and increase welfare expenditures. Proper management of aggregate demand and structural competition reduces the *total* amount of government intervention. Government is managing the economic environment in which the market operates, not the market itself.

We must not view the "business cycle" as an inevitable, self-generating feature of a capitalist economy in whose uncontrollable swings we are trapped. Significant economic fluctuations will certainly always be with us, but extended shortfalls of employment such as occurred in 2001–4 are simply unnecessary. They represent mistakes in management by previous or concurrent administrations. And certainly long inflationary periods like 1965–95 represent gross errors of judgment.

No one can possibly understand the working of the New Economy without recognizing the vast improvements that have been made in government management of both the demand side and the supply side of markets. Future progress requires a recognition of necessary changes yet to be made in the management of the market environment.

An examination of the record of demand management in the United States reveals three important facts:

• The United States has suffered mightily due to nonexistent or faulty demand management.

• The United States has learned a great deal about managing aggregate demand, *most of it recently*. That knowledge accounts for much of the improvement in economic performance we have experienced. It will surely bring a twenty-first century economic performance far superior to what prevailed in most of the past century.

• Two further improvements to demand management are needed, as described in Chapters 1 and 2.

The Banking System

For the first century and a half of its existence, the United States was plagued with a primitive banking system. It produced financial panics, waves of bank failures, and radically fluctuating demand leading to periods of high unemployment and low economic growth. Not until 1935 was a reasonably stable banking system established with deposit insurance and necessary regulation. Since then, waves of bank failures with their destabilizing impact on demand and the economy have been nonexistent. A reasonably stable banking system is a necessary foundation for effective management of aggregate demand.

Managing Demand in the Great Depression

The use of monetary and fiscal policy to manage aggregate demand was not even considered at the beginning of the Great Depression. Consequently, other objectives took precedence in decision making. Taxes were increased to meet the perceived need to balance the budget. Monetary policy was tightened to meet the perceived need to protect the dollar on the foreign exchange markets. Both policies depressed demand and exacerbated the depression. Later on, public pressures seeking relief from the ills of the Great Depression drove government to a moderate use of fiscal stimulus to strengthen demand. Late in the depression, the Keynesian revolution gave widely accepted intellectual support for even greater fiscal stimulation. But then came World War II. The problem of inadequate demand and depression gave way to the problem of excessive demand and inflation.

From World War II to 1965: Taming Inflation

The United States exited World War II with a burst of inflation created by pent-up demand due to wartime shortages of consumer goods and high consumer liquidity stemming from large accumulated savings. Until 1965, inflation control was high on the agenda of monetary and fiscal authorities cooperating to restrain total demand. Four recessions (1948–49, 1953–54, 1957–58, and 1960) were the penalties paid for the restraint on growth in demand. The resulting below-capacity competition was evidenced in the labor market by unemployment rising to between 5 and 7 1/2 percent in each recession. The unemployment rate showed a gentle upward trend from the end of the Korean War to 1961.

By 1961, low inflation expectations (wage norms in the labor market) were well established. As a reward for taming inflation, monetary authorities were able to allow faster growth for five years and still maintain low inflation and low unemployment. Worker compensation (wages plus benefits) grew quite steadily at around 4 percent a year, and consumer prices generally increased a little less than 2 percent a year. The unemployment rate gradually declined to about 4 percent. Productivity grew rapidly. The intensity of structural competition held reasonably steady over that five-year period. Perhaps stable wage norms were the most important part of the stable structural competition. The excellent economic performance of the first half of the 1960s had been earned by the disciplined management of demand in the 1950s. Then came the tragic Federal Reserve error of allowing inflation to accelerate. That error was accompanied by new impediments to structural competition. Together they launched the United States into an inflation binge that didn't peak until 1980 and took many years thereafter to heal as Chart 3.1 showed

Demand Management Over the Inflation Cycle, 1965–95

During the 1965–95 inflation cycle, the first blow to the effectiveness of competition in performing its function of restraining inflation was delivered by the Federal Reserve. In 1966, and for the following three years as the inflation rate accelerated, the Federal Reserve retreated from its responsibility to maintain price stability, a responsibility it had so carefully nurtured for the previous fifteen years. It allowed demand to grow so rapidly that output pushed up against capacity, eliminating necessary below-capacity competition. *Necessary* below-capacity competition is the amount of slack that allows markets to function effectively. In the labor market, unemployment (a measure of below-capacity competition) dropped below 4 percent in February 1966 and stayed there for four years. In the product market, industrial production rose to 90 percent of capacity, and in the important residential shelter market, rental vacancy rates dropped to the 5-to-6-percent range from the 7 1/2-to-8 1/2-percent range where they had stayed for several years. These three developments were important evidence of output pressing strongly against capacity, thereby largely eliminating below-capacity competition. Thus, because of the Federal Reserve neglect, a period of excessive inflation with all its unfortunate accoutrements was launched, not to be brought under control for more than a quarter of a century.

A great many people believe the inflation cycle was caused by the oil shocks. But the first oil shock came in late 1973, eight years after inflation began to accelerate, and the second oil shock came just a few months before inflation peaked in 1980, as shown in Chart 3.1. The oil shocks exacerbated inflation but certainly did not cause it. Various other factors weakened *structural* competition prior to the first oil shock, adding to the inflationary impact of the relaxed

Federal Reserve policy (more about this momentarily).

During the 1970s, the Federal Reserve twice made half-hearted attempts to bring inflation under control by monetary restraint. In 1970, and again in 1973–74, demand was curtailed, slowing output and bringing about the two moderate recessions of those years. But several impediments to *structural* competition had developed so much that moderate applications of below-capacity competition could not bring inflation down. (Most of the reduction in the inflation rate in 1971 and 1972 came in response to a short-lived attempt at wage and price controls.) By the late 1970s inflation had lasted so long and become so severe that the specter of runaway prices could not be totally dismissed. Fear was running high. The possibility of bringing inflation under control by severe monetary restraint raised the danger of another Great Depression.

Confusion about the management of monetary policy added to the fear engendered by other unsettling factors—accelerating inflation, the failure of wage and price controls, high unemployment, and oil shocks. In the late 1960s and the 1970s several members of the Open Market Committee and much of the Federal Reserve professional staff held an exaggerated interpretation of Keynesian economic theory. They downgraded monetary restraint in favor of fiscal restraint to curb inflation even though the Johnson administration in the 1960s was clearly laggard in its use of fiscal restraint. The minutes of the meetings of the Federal Reserve Open Market Committee reveal a deathly fear of triggering a recession. The fear of recession was much greater than the fear of ongoing accelerating inflation. The Committee, like much of the financial community, kept searching for that illusive measure of the money supply that could be used as an automatic guide to monetary policy. It was a hopeless task. There is no such dependable guide.

Finally, in 1980, Paul Volcker, the newly appointed chairman of the Federal Reserve Board, aggressively tightened money, thereby reducing demand and dramatically increasing below-capacity competition. It was necessary shock therapy, and it required extraordinary courage. Unemployment rose to nearly 11 percent and industrial capacity utilization dropped to nearly 70 percent. The inflation rate, of course, quickly declined as below-capacity competition increased. The economy embarked on a healing trend. By 1995 substantial strengthening of structural competition supplemented by reasonably moderate and judicial use of below-capacity competition had gradually brought the inflation rate back close to the level of the early 1960s. Mr. Volcker had taken one of the actions necessary to launch the New Economy.

And so thirty years of the last half century were marred by the inflation cycle initiated by that failure of the Federal Reserve to curb inflation in the late 1960s together with an increase in impediments to structural competition. Could the Federal Reserve error be repeated?

Bond Market Control of Inflation

The need for central banks to maintain the inflation rate at a low average and relatively steady rate appears to be thoroughly embedded in the minds of monetary authorities around much of the world. If the Federal Reserve should abandon this policy as it did in the late 1960s, the bond market would restrain inflation for them. Any serious evidence that the Federal Reserve was losing its inflation-fighting credibility would cause bond buyers to demand a greater inflation-risk premium in interest rates. Bond prices would fall, and stock prices would follow. As interest rates rose, the economy would slow and below-capacity competition would dampen inflation.

Why didn't bond buyers do this in the late 1960s and the 1970s? Because they believed that inflation was temporary, as it had always been. We know this because they were buying bonds at prices that would give them a satisfactory yield *only if the inflation rate dropped quickly*. Of course they were making a mistake. Bond buyers' mistakes in the late 1960s and the 1970s are understandable. Historically, periods of inflation had always been temporary, usually associated with wars. Bond buyers today are much more sophisticated. Those mistakes are not likely to be repeated.

The financial markets, then, have a kind of veto power over some government policies. If government adopts fiscal policies that appear to be inflationary, the financial markets will tumble, increasing interest rates and threatening recession. Therefore governments are reluctant to adopt such policies. This veto power over fiscal imprudence is well understood by government budget makers.

But an even greater power over inflationary goverment policy may lie ahead. In Chapter 4 we suggest that financial markets will soon begin to react negatively to new government *regulations whose compliance costs threaten inflation.* This inflation threat is more difficult to recognize, but it will become a much more common topic of discussion as the inflation cost of complying with new regulations becomes better known. And, as Chapter 4 argues, pressures on government to adopt inflationary social service regulations will be enormous, bringing the issue of compliance costs to our attention.

Evolution of the Management of Structural Competition

Any discussion of the supply-side factors that govern the effectiveness of structural competition in holding down prices and stimulating productivity must begin with a description of three powerful forces that have recently *improved* competition: increased international competition, reasonably effective antitrust enforcement and deregulation, and better opportunities for would-be competitors to gain access to capital and education.

Greater Commitment to International Trade

As everyone knows, a vast increase in competition in the manufacturing sector of the economy has followed the increased U.S. commitment to freer international trade. Two things should be noted about that increased competition. First, it is relatively new. The great bulk of it has occurred in the past twenty-five years, and it has accounted for much of the improved economic performance over that period. Second, the impact extends far beyond the manufacturing sector. Increased competition in one major sector of the economy helps to hold down costs and prices in other sectors. The slower growth in wage rates in the manufacturing sector has, by precedent, helped to reduce the growth of wages in other sectors.

Noisy demonstrations against global trade are frequently in the news. Small barriers to trade are frequently put in place. A tit-for-tat trade war always seems to be on the verge of breaking out. Could the U.S. commitment to international trade be reversed? As previously mentioned, the greatest danger is a prolonged period of high unemployment. That always raises demands to protect American workers from competition from low-paid foreign workers.

A significant decline in international trade would run up against a formidable obstacle—something we call the Geographic Law of Specialization: *the greater the variety of goods produced, the wider the trading area necessary to obtain adequate specialization.* In agricultural-handicraft economies, a trading area of just a few miles was adequate to find specialists for most of the limited items used. Today, the extensive variety of products requires a worldwide trading area to find specialists that can efficiently produce each of those products. The variety of desired and needed products will continue to increase. No country or group of countries will be able to find the specialists for efficient production without *extensive* trade beyond existing borders. A market needs *more than one specialist for each product.* It needs enough producers to provide a competitive discipline. The wide variety of products makes that impossible for any single country today.

Of course, very small reductions in international trade could be tolerated, but a major reduction would force countries to scramble to find domestic (less efficient) suppliers to replace imports. Those less-efficient domestic suppliers would inevitably be higher-cost producers. Competition would weaken. Inflation would quickly follow. Central bank restraint would be required to increase below-capacity competition to restrain prices. Unemployment would surge. We suspect that those adverse results would begin to appear quickly enough to cut short a major move to protectionism.

No free-trader should presume that barriers to international trade can be removed without pain. Laying off workers who have spent much of a lifetime in a particular job because they suddenly cannot meet the new competition from workers half a world away drawing a small fraction of the laid-off workers' pay, must be painful to all concerned. Furthermore, as we pointed out in Chapter 1, a large number of less-talented workers in the United States are currently paying a heavy price for the great benefits the rest of the country enjoys through increased international trade. The least we can do is provide a better employment environment with a flexible fiscal stimulus plan as described in Chapter 1.

Antitrust Enforcement and Deregulation

Reasonably aggressive antitrust enforcement and deregulation of some industries have also improved structural competition. A study by W. G. Shepherd concluded that between 1958 and 1980 industries generating 20.4 percent of national income moved from the pure monopoly, dominant firm, and tight oligopoly categories to become effectively competitive.[3] This left just 2.5 percent as pure monopoly, 2.8 percent as dominant firm, and 18.0 percent as tight oligopoly. *Antitrust enforcement and the threat thereof accounted for about half the shift to effective competition.* Economic deregulation and increases in international trade together accounted for the rest. Since the late 1970s other industries have been deregulated, most of which have successfully increased competition. The antitrust and deregulation improvements in competition that have already been achieved should continue well into the twenty-first century, although the vigor of antitrust enforcement varies moderately as administrations in Washington change. Large multinational companies are facing *increased* antitrust restraints. These companies are finding that they are subject to monopoly restraint in places other than their home countries. Witness the failure of General Electric's attempt to acquire Honeywell, which was prevented by European competition authorities.

Improved Opportunity to Compete

Improved availability of capital has expanded the opportunity to compete. Venture capital and the NASDAQ stock exchange have provided ready sources of funds that enable innovative young people to introduce new products and services without going through long periods climbing the corporate ladder. Also, employees in existing companies who are frustrated by the unwillingness of superiors to undertake promising new projects can leave the firm and find the capital to strike out on their own. The history of IT is replete with interesting stories of revolutionary products that were invented in established companies but were developed and made successful by employees who left the companies, raised the necessary capital, and started ventures on their own.

Greater opportunity for education has also added to the opportunity to compete. Financial barriers to higher education have been reduced. Opportunities for women and minorities to obtain better education have increased. Admission to some prestigious universities, whose graduates have often found their way into powerful positions in government and business, is now based somewhat more on merit than lineage. Openings to these routes to power are thereby expanded.

And so the opportunity to compete continues to spread as new people have access to investment capital and necessary education. One can only marvel at the impact on competition and productivity this major pillar supporting the New Economy will have as billions of people throughout the world gain the opportunity to compete in world markets in the coming century.

The recentness and magnitude of these various developments that have improved structural competition suggest that they have been important forces behind the blossoming of the New Economy. They should continue and improve well into the new century.

Impediments to Structural Competition

Those competition-enhancing forces just described have

substantially increased the intensity of structural competition over the past half century, but mainly over the past twenty-five years. Unfortunately, their benefits were delayed by major roadblocks beginning in the late 1960s. Those roadblocks were of two kinds. First, there was a series of impediments partly related to the War on Poverty and the Great Society programs. Those impediments were greatly intensified by the first oil shock in 1973. Second, the effects of impediments to structural competition were magnified by the previously described grievous error on the part of the Federal Reserve by which it temporarily abandoned, beginning in 1965, its responsibility to maintain stable prices. The combination of substantial impediments to structural competition and the failure of demand management produced the inflation cycle that began in 1965, peaked in 1980, and then took another fifteen years to heal, as discussed earlier.

The most remarkable *single* structural impediment of that fifteen-year upswing of the inflation cycle was the activation of the OPEC oil monopoly, which drastically reduced competition in one important industry. But although the oil shocks *exacerbated* the inflation problem, they did not *cause* it. That first oil shock came in late 1973, eight full years after the onset of the inflation cycle; the second came just a few months before the cycle peaked in 1980.

The inflation rate tripled from 1965 to just before the first oil shock in late 1973, indicating a substantial decline in the intensity of *overall* competition. Nevertheless, *below-capacity* competition (as measured by the capacity-utilization rate in manufacturing and the unemployment rate in the labor market) had actually strengthened by the time of the first oil shock. If overall competition weakened and below-capacity competition strengthened, then structural competition (the other part of overall competition) must have weakened substantially before the first oil shock. In fact, four other structural factors weakened overall competition:

1. *Costs of a third-party-payment health-care system.* In the past half century, the United States shifted from a reasonably competitive, private fee-for-service health-care system to a third-party-payment system in which the third parties are gov-

ernment and employer-financed insurance. This change moved a significant amount of decision making away from the discipline of competitive markets, thereby reducing structural competition and increasing health-care costs dramatically. When medical bills are paid by a third party, patients have little incentive to limit the quantity of services demanded or to search out the lowest-cost providers. Providers, in turn, often have little incentive to limit either the quantity of service provided or the prices charged. More often their personal incomes depend on increasing the quantity of service provided at higher charges.

The big surge in third-party payments came in the late 1960s with the establishment of Medicare and Medicaid, probably stimulating the rapid growth in private, employer-financed health insurance that had begun during World War II. Since the increased health-care costs affected most employers in much the same way, since they often came as a surprise, and since they came at a time when competition was weak, these costs were likely shifted to the consumer in higher prices rather than being shifted back to workers in the form of more slowly growing wages. The net result was a sharp increase in medical costs as a percentage of GDP and an intensification of inflation. Personal health-care expenditures rose from about 5 percent of GDP in 1966 to nearly 8 percent in 1980 and have continued to increase to about 14 percent today.

2. *The union wage premium.* Several studies have documented a sharp rise in the union wage premium in the early 1970s. This overriding of competition by unions in the labor markets was not due to any new legislation but was rather an activation of the latent power that unions had received from the 1935 National Labor Relations Act and the vast increase in union membership during and immediately following World War II. The limits to that union market power had not been tested in the 1950s and early 1960s.

3. *Social regulation.* The compliance costs of social regulation grew rapidly with the establishment of the War on Poverty and Great Society programs of the 1960s. Environmental legislation was the single most important part of this social legislation from the standpoint of the impact on compliance costs. Social regulation moved a great many cost decisions from the

jurisdiction of competitive markets to the jurisdiction of government and generally drove those costs higher. Therefore, the efficacy of structural competition was reduced.

4. *Reservation wages.* A reservation wage is a wage below which workers will choose to remain unemployed rather than work for less than that wage. A reservation wage can be changed substantially by changing the amount of unemployment insurance and/or welfare benefits to which the unemployed worker is entitled. During the late 1960s and part of the 1970s, both unemployment insurance and welfare benefits became substantially more attractive, giving workers an incentive to remain unemployed rather than competing in the labor market.

Data are not available to calculate with precision the effect each of those impediments had in limiting structural competition in the late 1960s and the 1970s. However, crude back-of-the-envelope type figuring leads us to believe that *in total* they had as much *direct* impact in impeding structural competition as did the two oil shocks. Since they started years prior to the first oil shock, they had a much greater *indirect* impact on inflation through the price-wage-price spiral than did the oil shocks. Consequently, they had a major effect in increasing the need for below-capacity competition with its undesirable unemployment.

So Much Accomplished—So Much to Be Done

In the management of aggregate demand, we have come a long way since those dark, inflationary days of the late 1960s and the 1970s. At that time the Federal Reserve was bogged down in enervating confusion (as was much of the financial community), searching for that illusive measure of the money supply that would serve as a single guide to direct the control of inflation. But even worse, the minutes of the Open Market Committee meetings indicate a continual timidity about restraining inflation for fear of pushing the country into a recession.

The Federal Reserve is now clearly dedicated to maintaining reasonable price stability and knows how to do it.

The long inflation cycle will not be repeated. If the Federal Reserve should neglect inflation control, the bond market would take control. Adoption of a supplemental flexible fiscal stimulus plan as described in Chapter 1 should be the next important step in the management of aggregate demand.

As this chapter has indicated, management of structural competition has also improved dramatically, but the learning process still has a long way to go. Future progress can be encompassed in one gigantic step. *The U.S. government must prominently and unequivocally assume the responsibility for maintaining structural competition sufficiently intense to hold inflation in check even at very low levels of unemployment, 4 percent or below.* This commitment is comprehensive in scope. It requires the continued nurturing of all the positive factors that sustain competition—international trade, effective antitrust enforcement, and support of all those features that smooth the way for new entrants into product, service, and labor markets. It also requires the elimination of thousands of impediments to the effective performance of competition in holding costs and prices down—impediments such as compliance costs of government regulations that we have described in this chapter. Elimination of these impediments must be a never-ending process.

To repeat, in a market economy, inflation will be controlled by competition. If not by structural competition, it will be controlled by below-capacity competition. The commitment to maintain intense structural competition basically states that we will restrain inflation by intense structural competition to avoid the need for below-capacity competition (unemployment) generated by restrictive monetary policy.

Whenever inflation creeps above the target of, say, 2 1/2 percent on the core CPI at a time when unemployment is above the target of 4 percent, we can no longer blame that inflation automatically on excessive demand created by monetary failures. We must look to weakness on the supply side—the structural competition side—of markets.

In Conclusion

Adequate, but not excessive, aggregate demand and intense structural competition are the two essential conditions for proper management of the market environment. Three policies are needed to provide those two essentials. The existing Federal Reserve price-stabilization policy together with a flexible fiscal-stimulus policy will provide adequate demand management. An active, ongoing policy of maintaining intense structural competition will ensure that demand is channeled into efficient production rather than into price increases. The three policies together will generate an evolving New Economy far better than anything ever witnessed any place in the world. We can learn to make this possible. One policy is in place. Two are yet to be adopted.

Chapter 4

MEETING GROWING DEMANDS FOR SOCIAL SERVICES

This may be the most important chapter in the book. Why? Because it deals with the policy of restraining inflation by maintaining intense structural competition. That is by far the most difficult of the three policies described in Chapter 3 that are necessary to maintain a rapid productivity growth rate and full employment coexistent with low inflation. This chapter also describes the coming titanic clash between rapidly growing demands for social services (including Social Security, Medicare, and environmental protection) and limited, painful ways of meeting those demands.

Social Service Needs

A competitive market can be harsh. If left entirely alone, it can be brutal. Every advanced country on Earth has taken steps to soften the results of competitive markets. Methods include progressive income taxes, public-financed education, labor unions, antitrust laws, welfare programs, retirement plans, health insurance, disability benefits, price controls, and trade protection. Every single one of these approaches to softening the results of competition has at one time or another been abused with a negative impact on human welfare. Nevertheless, elements of most of those programs are useful and will certainly continue.

The aging of the population and the growing complexity of human society will increase the demand for social services above its already high level. Social Security and Medicare alone are raising alarms that the trillions of dollars to be required will provoke a financial crisis soon unless changes in present policies are made.

Include the demands for environmental protection, especially with the specter of global warming possibly showing more immediacy, and the stage is set for heavy burdens to somehow be financed by government. How can those demands be met without triggering inflation or weakening the supply-side incentives and competition that make a market system work? This we believe will be the most important *economic* problem of the twenty-first century in the United States. Demands for social services will not go away. An administration that ignores those demands may be as vulnerable to the wrath of the electorate as an administration that provides the benefits but with excessive costs in taxes, unemployment, or inconvenience.

Social Service Wish Lists

We have read recent wish lists of a number of organizations that generally support increased social services. These organizations are generally politically powerful, but this power will be somewhat muted in a Republican-dominated government. Reading those wish lists is an astonishing experience. They are simply staggering in their enormity. In total their costs would amount to trillions of dollars.

Those organizations include labor unions, the Sierra Club, the American Association of Retired Persons, the Urban League, the American Association for the Advancement of Colored People, and the National Education Association. Their wish lists include literally dozens of programs to improve the health, income, job security, and retirement benefits of especially those who are elderly, sick, and poor, but really everyone. The wish lists also include improved support for the schools and increased protection of the environment. Most Americans would like to have some of the benefits provided by programs on the wish lists, but they are not anxious to bear the costs. Many of the initiatives in the wish lists have costs over and above the trillions of dollars of costs of benefits already promised aging Americans by existing Social Security and Medicare programs.

The organizations making the proposals seldom consider costs. Occasionally *cash* costs to government are estimated, but *practically never are the inflationary effects of compliance costs considered.* Effects of new programs on inflation and on the unemployment that follows are completely ignored.

Wages (and benefits) make up such a large part of the cost of economic activity that they demand special attention. Furthermore, the labor union wish lists were the most disturbing of all the wish lists we read. They call for changes in the law that would substantially improve unions' ability to organize and would strengthen their bargaining power in contract negotiation. Unions also propose changes in international trade agreements—changes that would restrict imports. Both of these initiatives would reduce competition and increase the union wage premium. These wage increases would push up prices. *And every dollar increase in the union wage premium represents a dollar less of inflationary compliance costs of new social services that can be tolerated.* Since a union wage premium is not necessary to attract qualified workers, cost-benefit comparisons between larger wage premiums and new social services will be overwhelmingly in favor of the new social services.

So that titanic struggle between rapidly growing demands and limited resources is being joined. How might it play out?

FOUR WAYS OF MEETING SOCIAL SERVICE COSTS

The following discussion of the four possible ways of meeting social service costs highlights the limited capability of government to meet those costs:

1. *Increasing taxes.* Increasing *income taxes substantially* will surely be near the bottom of the list of methods any administration will want to use to meet demands for social services. They are so unpopular. Yet some increase will likely be necessary. In any event, moderate income tax increases will be just a token step toward meeting all the social service demands. Other taxes are also unpopular. Taxes levied on business are often shifted (in part or entirely) on to consumers by increased prices. Upward pressure on prices adds to the need for Federal Reserve restraint with its slower growth and unemployment.

2. *Deficit financing.* Meeting cash expenditures by borrowing can be used in periods of recession and low inflation.

But if those increased deficits persist as the economy approaches full employment, they *may* create excessive aggregate demand and become inflationary. Of course, conditions throughout the economy such as changes in the saving rate or international capital flows *may* at times allow substantial government deficits to exist at full employment without creating inflation, but governments cannot rely on the persistence of such conditions. Government deficits at full employment generally carry the risk of creating excessive aggregate demand and inflation, to be followed by monetary restraint and rising unemployment. Deficit financing *cannot* be used reliably as a long-term solution for meeting the growing demands for social services.

3. *Business regulation.* Requiring business to bear the burden of social and environmental services may become a politically attractive alternative. This approach was used extensively by the Johnson administration's War on Poverty and Great Society programs. But if used currently the result will be far different from the result of that earlier experiment. New regulations will increase compliance costs now as they did then. Increased compliance costs will be passed on to the consumer in higher prices now as they were then. Inflation will accelerate now as it did then. But this time, accelerating inflation will be followed quickly by Federal Reserve restraint, a slowing economy, and rising unemployment. That did not happen under the Johnson administration because the Federal Reserve abdicated its responsibility to maintain stable prices. The penalty for cost-increasing regulations was postponed and magnified in the process. The Federal Reserve has learned from past experience. It will not fail again.

In a market-managed economy, inflation is restrained by competition. When government regulations increase compliance costs and thus impede the ability of structural competition to hold down prices, the Federal Reserve has to increase the intensity of below-capacity competition (unemployment) to supplement the weakened structural competition. So if the cost-enhancing regulation approach is used *aggressively* to satisfy social service demands, accelerating inflation, Federal Reserve restraint, and rising unemployment will follow.

Is there any way to prevent regulatory-induced inflation? Yes, there is—through the elimination of old regulations that have outlived their usefulness. By eliminating old regulations with their compliance costs, new regulations with equivalent compliance costs can be adopted without increasing *total* compliance costs. Together the two actions are inflation neutral. This approach opens up vast possibilities for improvement in government. If the Congress, under pressure to provide new services, should set up a workable, ongoing system to eliminate outmoded programs, it would take a monumental step toward improving the management of a democratic, capitalist economy. It would be able to adopt some new programs and still avoid the consequences of regulation-induced inflation. Much more about this later in this chapter.

4. *Other regulations*. Regulations can sometimes be crafted so that they will not significantly increase business compliance costs, but they generally carry other unpleasant consequences. For example, to reduce automobile carbon dioxide emissions (and conserve resources) government might limit the size of cars. Compliance costs would not intensify inflation, but the regulations would impose serious inconveniences on many consumers. Regulations that provide a social or environmental service without inflationary compliance costs or inconveniences to voters will be difficult (impossible?) to design.

Controlling Excessive Social Service Demands

Excessive populism is always a potential danger in a democracy. By excessive populism we mean the government practice of delivering so many social services to the public that they have a net negative impact. Those negative impacts include inflation, destruction of incentives to work and invest, and the buildup of burdensome debt. How can excessive social-service demands be controlled?

So far we have recognized the existence of *unavoidable*, growing demands for social services due to the aging of the population and the growing complexity of human society.

We have also recognized the voices of powerful groups that are pressing for major expansions of social services. And we have recognized the limitations on our ability to provide those services without damaging the economy that keeps people productively employed so that they don't need as many governmentally supplied social services.

In the face of powerful political pressures, how can we control the social-service function so that it does not do more harm than good? We have examined the four major ways by which the government can provide social services. The first, by increasing taxes on voters, has been fairly well controlled by tax revolts. It will likely continue to be so. The last, by regulations that impose inconveniences on voters, can be quite effectively controlled by the ballot box. Excessive use of the second approach—deficit financing—is now quite well controlled by the *threat* of inflation that precipitates unpopular declines in security markets. This is a control that has recently arisen through the learning process of both government officials and the investing public. Inflationary deficits, when the economy is near full employment, will likely be controlled.

That leaves the third approach described above, government regulations with compliance costs that impede the ability of structural competition to hold inflation down. This approach is dangerous because it is not properly understood by many government officials and legislators or by the public and thus is not easily controlled. That gap can be closed by the learning process.

The Necessity of Making Choices

At any one time there are limits to the amount of inflationary compliance costs that can be tolerated without triggering Federal Reserve monetary restraint followed by increased unemployment. These limits are real. They must be recognized. And when they are recognized they will make more vivid the trade-offs that are necessary in choosing social services.

Every additional dollar required for, say, environmental protection that increases inflationary compliance costs will reduce by a dollar the amount available for business-financed health care, or safety requirements for workers, or business services for the handicapped, or some other social service. Increased union bargaining power that increases the union wage premium will reduce the inflationary compliance costs of social services that we can tolerate.

The hope that increased compliance costs for many social services can be absorbed by reducing corporate profits is an illusion. Domestic corporate profits after tax (not adjusted for IVA and CCA) as a percentage of GDP have fluctuated mostly between four and five percent over the past decade. Not much if any of the compliance costs arising from increased social services could be absorbed by reducing corporate profits without destroying the ability of corporations to accumulate the investment capital necessary to keep the economy growing. That pesky term *inflationary compliance costs* must more and more intrude into economic and political discourse as debate develops over which social services we prefer within our limited resources.

Full Employment—The Basic Social Service

Almost all social services are more difficult to provide when the economy is operating below a full employment level of activity. Therefore, full employment can be considered the basic social service. Historically, unemployment has been a scourge that has afflicted all capitalist countries. The Great Depression provides the best-known example. We have learned a great deal about preventing or attenuating periods of serious unemployment, but threats to full employment still remain. We will consider three of them: the inadequate aggregate demand threat, the inflation threat, and the outsourcing threat.

The Inadequate Demand Threat to Full Employment

We have come a long way toward eliminating the problem of inadequate demand. But as described in Chapter 1, one particular situation can still give us trouble. Sometimes monetary stimulation, even when used to the fullest extent feasible, fails to adequately stimulate the economy. The 2001–4 period is a case in point. The flexible fiscal stimulus plan described in Chapter 1 provides a solution to the problem. As this is written in the fall of 2004, unemployment is still excessive. If the economy weakens further in 2005 additional fiscal stimulus should be applied immediately. The flexible fiscal stimulus plan is the only way *adequate* stimulation can be provided with the assurance that stimulation can be stopped quickly when no longer required.

Furthermore, the plan would be ready to protect against some future occurrence of inadequate aggregate demand when aggressive monetary policy is inadequate to provide sufficient stimulation. Such a situation may be close at hand. As we described in Chapter 1, and as a number of forecasters predict, a leveling off of the recent surge in home prices could bring a serious slowing in the growth of consumer spending. If it occurs, that flexible plan should be on the books ready for immediate implementation.

The Inflation Threat to Full Employment

In the years ahead we will face many inflation threats. Unless accelerating inflation is just moderately above target and is judged to be clearly due to some temporary factor, the monetary authorities should immediately apply restraint *without worrying about the cause of the inflation.* If that inflation is due to excessive aggregate demand, it will quickly be brought under control and monetary restraint can be relaxed as the growth of demand slows and as the inflation threat recedes. The experience of 1994 is a case in point. A minor acceleration of inflation was easily brought under control by monetary restraint. That 1994 experience was a successful example of monetary fine-tuning of the economy.

But if inflation is due to weak structural competition, the problem is more serious. If monetary restraint slows the economy *but inflation persists*, the cause of that inflation is not excessive aggregate demand, but rather *impediments that limit the ability of competition built into the structure of the economy to hold prices down.* Above-target unemployment coexistent with above-target inflation is evidence of weak structural competition. In this case monetary restraint should, and will, be continued until inflation is subdued even though the economy remains sluggish and unemployment is excessive. Steps must be taken to remove the impediments that are reducing the ability of structural competition to restrain inflation. That often takes considerable time, so by far the best policy is to avoid allowing those impediments to arise.

A great danger lies in the fact that many people, in and out of the government, seem to be unaware of the impact of increased compliance costs of legislation in restraining the ability of structural competition to hold down inflation. An awareness of the impact on unemployment of programs that boost costs and prices is one of the learning processes that is not yet complete. Any program that allows, or causes, prices to rise is a job destroyer.

The Outsourcing Threat to Full Employment

Most Americans are concerned about the loss of American jobs to overseas competition. The United States is buying from abroad about half a trillion dollars a year more goods and services than we are selling there. As a consequence, foreigners now own about three trillion dollars more of U.S. assets than Americans own of foreign assets. We cannot go on for long with such a large adverse trade balance.

Our adverse trade balance would normally be corrected by a drop in the value of the dollar on the foreign exchange market. That would make imports more expensive to local buyers and exports less expensive to foreign buyers. Imports would decline, exports would rise, and the adverse balance of trade would be corrected. Why has the dollar not dropped far enough to correct the trade balance? Over the last several years the dollar has held up against other currencies in real terms due to the success of the American economy. Foreign individuals, companies, and governments have bought dollars to buy American companies, common stocks, real estate, and debt instruments. They have also considered the United States dollar a low-risk investment as compared to many other currencies. Furthermore, the American economy is so large that dollar investments are highly liquid. They can be bought and sold quickly in large quantities.

But recently a more provocative force has kept the dollar high. Japan, China, and other countries won't let it fall. They keep buying dollars to support its price, and then they invest those dollars in U.S. government securities. Japan now owns about 15 to 20 percent of all U.S. government obligations not held by U.S. government entities. China also has large and growing holdings. Japan and other countries want to keep the price of their currencies low so they won't lose their export markets.

What should the United States do? Unless inflation accelerates sharply, we should use the flexible fiscal stimulus plan outlined in Chapter 1 to get closer to full employment without further delay. That won't solve the balance-of-trade problem, but it will likely prevent our using that problem as an excuse for adopting unwise policies such as building long-term barriers to imports. Workers who have lost jobs because of imports will at least have the chance of getting a job in another industry. Full employment reduces the insecurity engendered by adverse trade balances.

How will the trade gap be closed? It will begin to close (with a lag) when other countries reduce their buying of dollars on the foreign exchange market. When will that happen? When those countries finally realize that it is to their advantage to allow the dollar to weaken much more. As this is written in the fall of 2004, China appears to be on the verge of allowing the yuan to rise in relation to the dollar. This action will allow China to buy fuel and other materials more cheaply, and its exports will command higher prices abroad—that is, its "terms of trade" will improve. It will be able to buy more imports with the same quantity of exports. Furthermore, it will dampen China's overheating economy. A rise in the value of the yuan in relation to the dollar will allow the currencies of other countries closely associated with China to rise against the dollar. China knows that its currency must sooner or later rise. It also knows that it will ultimately take a loss on many of those over-priced dollar-denominated assets it is now buying. That knowledge should encourage China to slow its dollar purchases soon.

Japan poses a more complex problem. For over a decade Japan's economy has been stagnant due to a horrendous decline in equity and real estate prices that has dramatically reduced the buying power of its consumers. Japan is afraid that a rise in the yen will slow its exports and thus choke off its modest recovery. Japan has many problems (as does every country), but inadequate aggregate demand is chief among them. Whenever a country has *no inflation problem coexistent with slow growth and above-target unemployment*, the problem is inadequate demand. And when a country has inadequate demand coexistent with a *surplus of production capacity and low interest rates*, the only way the economy can be stimulated is by government fiscal policy. Japan has tried the stimulus of government deficit spending but never sufficiently to achieve a sustained recovery. Japan needs its own version of the flexible fiscal stimulus plan outlined in Chapter 1. It can be used *aggressively* as needed to initiate a sustained recovery and then slowed and stopped when recovery is assured.

As the dollar declines on foreign exchange markets, and as the United States imports diminish, each country will need to offset the loss of exports by stimulating its own economy. The stimulus required will depend upon the conditions in each country. A country that has above-target inflation and also above-target unemployment has structural competition that is too weak to hold prices down. While (or before) stimulating its economy, that country must go through the arduous process of increasing that built-in competition, a difficult and often lengthy undertaking.

Is a crisis likely to come from Japan, China, or other countries *suddenly* selling their U.S. government securities, causing a *precipitous* drop in the dollar and raising U.S. interest rates? These countries have a great interest in preventing such a crisis because a precipitous drop in the dollar would cripple their export markets. They will desperately want to avoid that and will try to engineer a gradual drop in the dollar against their currencies. Nevertheless, the highly speculative foreign exchange markets often have sharp, erratic moves.

We cannot be sure that the downward adjustment of the dollar will be smooth.

The United States must be aware of an adverse consequence of a declining dollar. It will increase import prices, exacerbating inflation directly. Furthermore, it will have a secondary impact on inflation. Rising import prices will reduce competition to local producers allowing their prices to rise. A *gradual* decline of the dollar will be to the advantage of both the United States and the rest of the world.

Despite our existing adverse trade balance, the future of the U.S. economy is still under reasonable control. It comes down to those two basic factors described in Chapter 3: maintain adequate but not excessive aggregate demand and intense structural competition. We have learned a lot about how to do that, and we are still learning.

Meeting Social Security Needs

As countless pundits continually assert, in a few years Social Security will face cash shortfalls as the baby boomers retire. As this is written in late 2004 the President is expected to propose a major change in the Social Security system allowing young workers to direct part of their Social Security taxes into personal retirement accounts over which they will have some degree of management authority. Details of the plan have not yet been worked out. But nearby cash shortfalls are apparently to be met by the borrowing of one or two trillion dollars. Proponents of the plan say that *long-term* cash shortfalls will be solved, but no details have yet been released as to how that will be accomplished.

If the partial privatization of Social Security becomes law, it will set the direction of Social Security for many years. It cannot easily be reversed. But powerful forces are being marshaled against it. The likelihood of its being enacted is not great. Several variations of the plan are apparently being developed. Debate on the bill could well be prolonged and become a critical issue in 2006 congressional elections.

If partial privatization fails, we will be back to square one, searching for a solution to the cash shortfall problem. So far we have not failed to solve our coming Social Security cash shortfall problem due to a want of workable solutions. We have failed due to an unwillingness to set up a workable *procedure* for arriving at a compromise solution that can be accepted by competing factions who have little interest in compromise. This problem of achieving a solution among disagreeing factions is a problem endemic to democratic government. The *delegation approach* has been used occasionally to achieve workable solutions. An independent commission, usually composed of bipartisan experts and legislators, is set up to arrive at an answer to a problem that has defied solution. A single solution is presented to Congress for an up or down vote *without the opportunity for amendment.* This takes the design details away from a contentious legislature. The delegation approach has been used in a number of intractable cases–closing military bases and writing trade agreements. *The delegation approach appears to be effective only when other approaches have been tried and failed, and when a solution is urgently needed.* Those conditions are approaching as the Social Security cash shortfall looms larger.

The delegation approach has already been used to meet a Social Security crisis. The National Commission on Social Security Reform, also known as the Greenspan Commission, was established by an executive order in December 1981. Social Security faced a serious financial crisis, and despite many different proposals, Congress had been unable to pass legislation to solve the problem. President Reagan, in order to "remove Social Security once and for all from politics," appointed five members to the commission. He also asked the Senate majority leader and the Speaker of the House to appoint five members each. The fifteen members represented both parties and about half of them were "experts," while the other half were members of Congress. President Reagan's goal was to "forge a working, bipartisan consensus so that the necessary reforms can be passed into law."[4]

About a year later, in January 1983, the commission presented a formal recommendation—a package of proposals—to the president and Congress. The recommendation left a couple of questions unanswered, but President Reagan expressed a desire to avoid making major changes or recommending specific answers. He did not want to interfere with the delicate balance of the commission's package.

President Reagan included the commission's recommendation, unchanged, in his budget proposal. Both houses of Congress also wrote the recommendation into bills. The bills were then amended in the subcommittees and committees, with some of the commission's specific proposals being accepted and others rejected. The final debate on the House floor *did not allow amendments*, and the bill passed as it had been reported by the committees. The Senate, however, allowed amendments even on the floor. The two bills were reconciled into one and signed by President Reagan on April 20, 1983.

President George W. Bush also established a commission on Social Security problems. It produced three possible solutions. This was a useful process, but it was not sufficient to force a decision upon competing factions. To do that, a *single* solution must be proposed, designed by bipartisan experts and legislators. Legislators are then forced, in an up or down vote, to make a stark choice between accepting the compromise or starting all over again to devise a solution to a problem that is becoming more and more urgent. Compromises do not come easily to competing factions.

If partial privatization fails, a new bipartisan commission should be appointed with instructions to produce a *single* recommendation that will be presented to Congress for an up or down vote. Rectifying the coming cash shortfall in our Social Security system will not be painless. A commission would likely recommend some combination of the following four changes:

• Improve the CPI escalator so that it doesn't overstate the inflation rate to which Social Security payments are tied.

• Reduce benefits, probably by reducing the growth rate of benefits received by new retirees. Those initial benefits to *new retirees* now grow faster than the CPI.

• Extend the retirement age again. It is already scheduled to rise to 67.

• Increase taxes on both employers and employees. Taxes on employers will be partly shifted to consumers through rising prices and will reduce the amount of inflationary compliance costs that can be tolerated from other programs.

To repeat, we have not failed to solve the coming cash shortfall in our Social Security system due to a want of workable solutions. We have failed, so far, to solve the problem due to an unwillingness to set up a workable *procedure* for arriving at a compromise solution. Some changes in our Social Security system will ultimately be required, but these changes are not nearly as urgent as changes in our health care system, a subject to which we will now turn.

Meeting Health Care Needs

The health care problem will be much more difficult to solve than the Social Security problem because it involves the entire third-party-payment health care system in the United States. That system is broken. It has at least five failings:

1. The system is awash with waste and fraud. Medical professionals often prescribe unnecessary procedures and charge too much, in part because their incomes often depend on the amount and price of those services. The cost puts little burden on the patients they are trying to please. Medical professionals also practice *defensive medicine*, prescribing extensive tests and procedures to protect against malpractice suits.

2. Patients demand unnecessary services because those services cost little or nothing.

3. Medicare and private insurers require huge amounts of costly overhead spending to try to limit the amount of services provided and the prices charged. Controlling waste and fraud is an ongoing, expensive problem. Medical personnel face heavy costs in complying with those controls.

4. Many people are not covered by the insurance system even though they pay some of the costs of medical insurance enjoyed by others. An indeterminate amount (possibly significant) of Medicare's hospitalization payroll tax paid by employers is shifted on to consumers and is paid by everyone in their daily purchases. The same can be said for employee health insurance paid by employers. Also uninsured people are putting an ever-growing burden on Medicaid.

5. Those who do not have insurance coverage through their employers pay for their medical services with after-tax dollars, in contrast with medical services obtained through employer-financed insurance. This problem is being moderated by the health savings account program.

The last two of these five problem areas weigh heavily on those who are often least able to bear the costs. Something must be done. Our broken system will not be easy to fix. But we must try. The aging population will soon make its failings intolerable. Fixing the third-party-payment system must begin with a mechanism for controlling excessive patient demands and excessive procedures authorized by medical professionals. Medicare currently attempts this control by tens of thousands of pages of regulations. These controls are very expensive and they don't work well.

The following principles should guide in designing a new health care system to correct those five failings:

Payment by capitation, not fee for service: When health care providers are paid for *each patient cared for* and not for *each service rendered*, the temptation to provide excessive services disappears. Providers have an incentive to hold costs down. They become more cost conscious. Thus, the first of the five failings is eliminated. A basic, no-frills, capitation plan should be the cost-setting standard for our health-care insurance system. Coverage (medical, dental, pharmacy, or other services) would be set periodically by government medical authorities. But a capitation plan of this kind has often been unpopular, and patients have demanded more extensive services such as options to select a physician, or the privilege of consulting more specialists, or the comfort from more frequent doctor visits. These demands lead to the second guiding principle.

Free access to health care must be limited: Unlimited access to food, clothing, housing, electricity, health care, or anything else leads to overuse and waste. As previously indicated, Medicare attempts to limit access to health care by tens of thousands of pages of regulations. That attempt is costly, unpleasant, often arbitrary, and not very effective. Patients have a wide variety of needs. They should have the right to choose from a variety of plans beyond the basic, no-frills, capitation plans, but not without discipline. That discipline should come from the necessity for the patient to pay insurance costs above the basic, no-frills, capitation plan. The patient judges whether the needs warrant paying the extra costs. The cost to employers of any plan offered as part of employee compensation above the basic, no-frills, capitation plan would not be deductible for tax purposes.

A second discipline in both basic and extended plans would come from a requirement that patients pay deductibles and co-payments for each service. Deductibles and co-payments have been shown to reduce patient demand without harming health outcomes.

The right of immediate appeal: Conflicts will always arise as to what services should be provided under any plan. Patients must have the right of *immediate* appeal to a medical review board, and must be able to expect a quick response. Malpractice costs must be contained for obvious reasons.

Universal insurance coverage: All employers above a certain size would be required to provide basic, no-frills, capitation insurance with substantial deductibles and co-payments. This insurance would be quite inexpensive. With substantial deductibles and co-payments, it would be directed mainly toward protection against serious, expensive treatments. Those not covered by employer-provided insurance or Medicare would have the basic insurance subsidized by government. Such extended coverage would sharply reduce the cost of the *Medicaid* program. But Medicaid would still survive. It would be required sometimes to pay deductibles and co-payments for those who qualify under "needs" and "means" tests. Some people will fall through the cracks of any system. Those people will come under Medicaid's responsibility.

What would the financial impacts be? Employers now paying for expensive insurance would reduce paid coverage to that of the no-frills coverage since the amount above the no-frills premium would not be tax-deductible. In competitive industries (and most are competitive) the employer would need to offset the reduction in health benefits by increasing (tax deductible) wages and salaries to remain a competitive employer. Employees who chose the no-frills plan would therefore see a rise in income. Employees who chose a more expensive plan would find themselves paying the higher premiums with after-tax dollars.

Employers larger than the designated size limit who currently offer no insurance would be required to offer the no-frills package. This extra cost would likely be offset in part by an initial reduction in wages or by slower-growing future wages. Part would likely be shifted forward in increased prices.

As for government, Medicare costs would drop sharply as government would pay only for no-frills insurance. Beneficiaries who chose to continue their present more elaborate policies would have to pay the amount above the cost of the no-frills policy. Most beneficiaries would find this objectionable, and this adjustment might have to be phased in gradually. But Medicare cannot go many years subsidizing the present elaborate health system. Government costs of insuring the presently uninsured would, of course, be significant even for no-frills, capitation insurance with substantial co-payments. Medicaid, which is currently headed for a financial disaster, would find major cost reductions as no-frills health insurance became universal.

Competition in Health-Care Services

Why has competition among hospitals, physicians, and insurance plans failed to eliminate waste and fraud and to rein in the rapid growth of services that is eating up a larger and larger share of our national output, currently about 15 percent? Competition has not been effective because it takes a peculiar twist under our third-party-payment system.

Ordinarily sellers in a market economy compete to attract consumers in two ways—by holding prices down and by improving services (quality of products). But in a third-party-payment system the seller has two customers to please: the patient who receives the service and the business or government that pays for the service. Circumstances have conspired to make the voice of the patient desiring more and better services more powerful than the voice of the employer or government trying to hold down the cost of the medical plan.

The decision to provide a service is made when the doctor meets the patient. To the doctor the most important goal is to retain the patient. It is usually more important than the general instructions of the plan's administrator to keep costs down. Not only must the doctor retain the patient, but he must avoid having dissatisfied patients complaining to their employers who choose which plan to buy. Furthermore, the doctor often relies on patient word-of-mouth advertising to build a clientele.

On the cost side, health plans must compete on a price basis. Employers need to hold prices down, but that need is somewhat ameliorated by the fact that the cost of the plan is tax deductible, can sometimes be partly shifted on to the consumer in higher prices, and frequently can be shifted back to the employee in slower wage increases. The upshot then is that competition among doctors to deliver more and better services is more powerful than the competition among plans to keep the total cost of health service down. And that differential in the power of the two types of competition may account for the fact that even organizations like Kaiser Permanente (one of the most efficient health organizations in the country operating on a capitation basis) finds itself involved in the upward creep of services provided and the total cost of those services.

The history of the third-party-payment system demonstrates the power of patient demands to drive up the amount and costs of services. For example, during the mid-1990s, HMOs using the capitation approach grew rapidly and held health-care costs to a very slow growth rate for a few years. But soon patients clamored for greater services such as choice of doctors, more frequent visits, and greater access to specialists. To satisfy patients, HMOs began creating less restrictive managed-care plans that allowed more consumer choice. Costs immediately started rising. Recently they have risen at frightening rates. Health outcomes do not appear to have improved with the more expensive system.

To reduce the imbalance between the power of price and service competition, several steps could be taken. The use of deductibles and co-payments could be expanded. Those payments require the patient to pay more attention to the price of the service. Even more important, when substantial co-payments are required, the doctor knows he is putting a cost burden on the patient he is trying to please when he prescribes a drug or a medical procedure. The doctor is, theoretically, in the best position to balance costs and benefits when prescribing a drug or medical procedure. But when the cost appears as just an ephemeral speck in the total cost of a large insurance plan he will usually emphasize the benefit to the real live patient he is trying to please. Consequently, total medical services delivered by the plan continue to escalate. If, however, the cost includes a substantial amount of co-payment paid by the patient, the doctor will give cost a somewhat greater weight in making the cost-benefit judgment.

As for tax deductibility, if costs above that of a no-frills, capitation insurance plan were not tax deductible, the employer would be encouraged to pay a greater part of employee compensation as (tax deductible) wages rather than as health benefits. Employees who chose elaborate plans would be forced to recognize the costs of the more expensive plans—costs that they would have to bear.

Steps to rectify the imbalance between price and service competition will have to be taken gradually. Health-care experts will be able to work out a better and more politically feasible health-care program than we have suggested. But any program that does not address the five failings described above is just skirting around the edges. Remember the prize. Any slowing of inflationary pressure on health-care costs will make possible a lesser need for below-capacity competition with its unpleasant unemployment. Or, alternatively, less inflationary pressure from health-care costs will make possible the adoption of other social services with their inflationary costs. Remember also the cost of inaction. The aging of the population will soon boost the growth of Medicare and Medicaid costs far above their current level, making the containment of inflation without the use of extensive below-capacity competition much more difficult.

Another aspect of competition is important. Competition never works well unless buyers and sellers have good information about price and quality of services. Governments have been woefully laggard in doing the research that would allow them to provide accurate guidelines to physicians and patients on the relative costs and effectiveness of various drugs and medical procedures. Such information would give the physician support in providing less-costly drugs and medical procedures without running the risk of malpractice suits.

Eliminating Old Programs to Make Room for New Ones

We can't have everything we want. By eliminating old government programs with their cash expenditures and compliance costs, we can introduce new and better programs with their cash expenditures and compliance costs without increasing total budget expenditures or aggravating inflation. Past attempts to eliminate tired old programs that have outlived their usefulness have foundered on *lack of time and expertise* on the part of legislators. Also, it is a thankless job. Special interest groups lobby to keep the old programs alive, but no lobbyists push to have them discontinued. That may change when the adoption of new programs is related to eliminating old programs.

The delegation approach to designing legislation might also be used to eliminate old programs. A commission of experts (including legislators) should be appointed to prepare a list of questionable existing programs, analyze them, and submit a batch of them to Congress each year for elimination or modification in an up or down vote without the possibility of amendment. The existing body of government programs should be viewed as a giant regulatory gold mine that can be exploited to make room for new and better programs with their cash expenditures and inflationary compliance costs. Virtually everyone agrees that a great many existing programs are of little value and should be eliminated or modified. We have no illusion that the "delegation" approach will always work, but as a last resort it ought to be tried. At least it might help to keep alive recognition of the need for constant reexamination of old programs.

Every dollar saved in cash expenditure or inflationary compliance costs will allow a dollar of cash expenditure or compliance cost of new and better programs. That should be an incentive to act.

Securities Markets May Limit Passage of Inflationary Regulations

Pressures from securities markets may actually *prevent* the adoption of some inflationary regulations. Securities markets already exercise considerable control over federal *fiscal* policy. Tax and spending proposals that appear to be inflationary often spook the bond and stock markets (except in time of recession). Declines in those markets (or even just fears that the markets will decline) sometimes prevent the passage of inflationary *fiscal* measures. Is it possible that regulatory proposals for social services that will intensify inflation by increasing compliance costs might also unsettle the securities markets and thus deter their passage?

Pressure on governments to keep unemployment low will likely keep the economy near full employment most of the time. Little bouts of inflation will be frequent. The danger of intensifying inflation will always be present. We suspect that inflationary aspects of social programs *due to increased compliance costs of regulation* will be increasingly recognized by economists in the financial sector. New regulatory proposals that appear to be inflationary will hurt the markets. One can easily imagine the impact that a hundred market strategists would have as they warned bond and stock investors of the inflationary impact of the compliance costs of a series of legislative proposals. Thus, the fear of adverse market reactions may deter the passage of some irresponsible proposals. Some market control of social service proposals may be coming.

Once again the learning process is involved. Analysts, bond and stock holders, and governments must learn to recognize the impact on inflation and unemployment that follows legislation that pushes costs upward, thereby restraining the power of structural competition to hold down inflation.

Productivity to the Rescue

Restraints on the ability of government to meet the growing demands for social services are not quite as tight as this chapter has, so far, portrayed. In Chapter 6 we argue that New Economy conditions will likely insure that the United States will achieve an average productivity growth rate (output per worker hour) of 2 1/2 to 3 percent far into the future. Adding a 1 percent growth in the labor force suggests a real growth of 3 1/2 to 4 percent. The amount spent on social services can grow at the same rate in inflation-adjusted terms if the *proportion* of national output spent on social services remains the same. If a half percentage point of that real growth could be diverted to increased social services, an *extra* fifty billion dollars or so in inflation-adjusted terms could be devoted to new social services *each year*.

To accomplish this diversion, incomes of other recipients would have to increase less than if they were getting the full benefit of their share of the increase in real growth. Then the government could increase cost-enhancing regulations an equivalent amount without boosting the inflation rate. Intense competition in the labor market and restraint on the part of powerful labor unions would be required to keep the wage rate growing slowly. Also, intense competition in product markets would be required to force business firms to hold down both wages and profits. Intense competition is still the key to the proper performance of the New Economy.

With an annual growth of 2 1/2 percent in productivity, hourly income of the average worker adjusted for inflation will double in about thirty years and quadruple in sixty years. With that kind of income growth, could we conceivably *not* find the resources to fund basic, no-frills health insurance for everyone and meet the demands for other social services due to the aging of the population and the growing complexity of society? Expected productivity growth is not a license for profligacy, but it should encourage us to face our need for social services with confidence that we can do better than we have done in the past.

We can look at growth in another way—the size of the spending-income stream as measured by *nominal* GDP. Currently that spending-income stream is measured at about 11 trillion dollars each year. At an annual growth rate of 6 percent it will double every twelve years, reaching about 22 trillion dollars in twelve years, 44 trillion dollars in twenty-four years, 88 trillion in thirty-six years, and 176 trillion dollars in forty-eight years. From that spending-income stream we should be able to extract sufficient funds to properly manage the social-service aspect of the New Economy.

What If We Should Take Cost-Benefit Analysis Seriously?

Now let's try to visualize what might happen if Americans were to take very seriously the question of both cash costs and inflation costs and relate them to benefits over a very wide range of activities. Vast opportunities are available for cutting costs of existing programs to make way for new programs. By just describing the following three possibilities we will certainly raise the ire of many very good people in this country. But we cannot have everything. Choosing wisely requires that we look at all possibilities for saving.

1. *Costs and benefits of extending individual lives*. Not surprisingly, medical costs for an individual are usually greatest in the last year of life. That is also often true for the last few days and hours of a person's life. How extensively should we use modern technology to prolong life? Medical professionals are faced with that decision daily. Many lives could be extended longer than we currently extend them by ventilators, intravenous feeding, and other procedures, but the benefit is not worth the cost. Now suppose we make an effort to withhold those treatments *far sooner* than we now do as the prognosis becomes more hopeless and the quality of life cannot be improved. Every dollar saved by withholding life-extending treatment in hopeless cases can be used to extend life and

improve the quality of life in other cases without adding inflationary pressure to the health care system—pressure that leads to increased costs, prices, and eventually Federal Reserve restraint and unemployment. The medical profession appears to be moving in that direction, but apparently huge amounts could still be saved. Medical authorities should provide guidelines describing procedures that are *not* appropriate to extend life in terminal cases.

A sudden, massive shift toward withholding life-extending treatments in terminal cases is not likely. But gradual movement in that direction is possible as the realization sinks in that such withholding can make possible the provision of more valuable services to other patients without increasing total cash outlays or inflationary pressure. The term *inflationary compliance costs* must be recognized throughout the entire medical establishment.

2. *Costs and benefits of union power.* Labor unions are monopolistic organizations. Their monopolistic power derives from an exemption from the antitrust laws that are designed to protect the public against competition-inhibiting market power. Union workers receive higher pay and better benefits than similarly qualified nonunion workers doing the same work. That differential is called the union wage premium. Union workers make up less than one-tenth of the private sector labor force and about one-third of government employees. In some cases unions prevent the adoption of modern labor-saving technologies that would significantly reduce the number of workers required and cut total labor costs. The highly publicized West Coast dock strike in 2002 is a case in point.

If the monopolistic power of labor unions were reduced or eliminated, *substantial* production cost saving would follow. The ability of structural competition to hold down prices would be enhanced. Less below-capacity competition would be required to restrain inflation, and unemployment would decline. Or, alternatively, some of the important social services now being neglected could be adopted even though they increase compliance costs.

Many worker rights such as protection from arbitrary firing formerly ensured only by unions are now ensured by law.

What are the *benefits* from union power that still justify their cost-increasing impact on inflation that forces greater application of below-capacity competition with its increased unemployment?

3. *Costs and benefits of the Endangered Species Act.* The U.S. Fish and Wildlife Service is required to maintain a list of threatened and endangered species. The service is specifically directed to *not* consider economic costs in deciding to put a species on that list. However, costs can be considered when promulgating rules on how to protect the species. Placing a species on the endangered list often increases costs to some industry, resulting in upward pressure on inflation. That pressure brings closer the Federal Reserve restraint that brings higher unemployment. Of course, the impact of protecting a single species would not be a defining factor in determining the inflation rate. But the impact of the entire program must be considered along with a thousand other inflationary regulations. Together they are important.

Making any decision without considering costs seems absurd. Ignoring costs, especially inflationary compliance costs, is the kind of mind-set that builds up inflationary pressure across the economy, leading to excessive unemployment or alternatively to the inability to adopt some other social service with its inflationary compliance cost. All species are not equal in importance. The service should be required to prepare an economic impact statement to justify placing a particular species on the endangered list. The *economic* costs should be justified by a description of the benefits the preservation of that particular species would provide.

In Conclusion

For decades many people have been repeating a kind of mantra: inflation is always and everywhere a monetary phenomenon. In an extremely narrow sense it is correct. Monetary restraint should be used to curb inflation. When inflation occurs it is, therefore, due to the *failure* to use monetary restraint, and so inflation is, in a sense, a monetary phenomenon. Unfortunately the mantra has often been used to claim that monetary excesses are always the *cause* of inflation. We must clearly disavow that notion. Now that monetary-induced (or allowed) inflation is being largely controlled, we must more often look to the supply side, the structural-competition side, of markets to recognize the cause of inflation and also its cure.

That critical policy described in Chapter 3 for inflation control must become a central guide for the evolving New Economy. To repeat, *the U.S. government must prominently and unequivocally assume the responsibility for maintaining structural competition sufficiently intense to hold inflation in check even at very low levels of unemployment, 4 percent or below*. And there is no place where the implementation of that policy is more important than in meeting the growing demand for social services.

Chapter 5

HAVE TAX DISINCENTIVES RESTRAINED GROWTH?

Have high tax rates been disincentives to work, save, and invest, thereby weakening the structural competition necessary to direct increasing aggregate demand toward increased production rather than increased prices? The need for cutting taxes to improve incentives to work, save, and invest has dominated fiscal policy debate the past few years. The incentive issue therefore deserves a chapter of its own even though it is a short one.

EFFECTS OF THE 1981 AND 1993 TAX RATE CHANGES

Fortunately, in the last quarter century we have had a major income tax cut (the 1981 Reagan cut) and a major income tax increase (the 1993 Clinton increase) to help us judge the impact of changing tax rates. How did the economy respond to these two events? In both cases a decade of rapid economic growth followed. (The Reagan tax cut came in the early stages of a sharp recession that was engineered by the Federal Reserve to break dangerously accelerating inflation.) The fact that a vigorous economic recovery followed both the tax cut and the tax increase suggests that the tax changes were not the *dominant* forces involved in those decade-long expansions. If the Reagan tax *cuts* were the primary cause of the economic advance of the 1980s, shouldn't the Clinton tax *increases* have derailed the economic advance of the 1990s? Several prominent supply siders believed it would happen. At the time of the Clinton tax increase, Rush Limbaugh offered to bet the Democratic National Committee one million dollars that, in essence, the United States would soon fall into a recession. He was voicing the opinion of supply siders that a major tax increase would reduce incentives to invest to such an extent that it would derail the recovery. They were, of course, wrong.

But how about the incentive effects of the rate changes on *specific* economic activities such as spending for capital investment? Chart 5.1 shows nonresidential fixed investment as a percentage of GDP. In the long economic recovery after

Chart 5.1 Nonresidential Fixed Investment as a Percentage of GDP

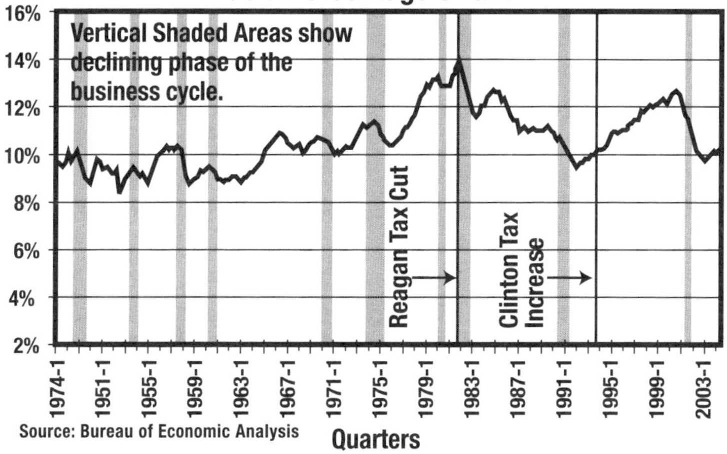

Source: Bureau of Economic Analysis

the Reagan tax cut, fixed investment spending grew more slowly than GDP, implying that capital spending *followed* rather than *led* the recovery. In the long economic recovery after the Clinton tax increase, capital spending grew faster than GDP, implying that capital spending led rather than *followed* the recovery. These two performances do not support the view that cuts in marginal income tax rates improve incentives to invest in plant and equipment. We made similar comparisons with industry-financed spending for R&D, new business starts, the employment-participation rate, and the saving rate. All four of these variables changed about the same amount after the Clinton tax increase as after the Reagan tax cut. Again these comparisons fail to support the view that tax cuts provide a special supply-side incentive for favorable economic activity.

The evidence we have cited so far does not support the idea of a *dominant* influence of supply-side tax-cut incentives on these economic variables. But neither does it indicate that the tax cuts had *no* effect. They may have had some effect that was overwhelmed by other factors. Certainly, taxes affect incentives. The question is how much at what rates? In any event the experiences just cited do not provide a ringing endorsement for the supply-side notion that moderate tax cuts provide a *major* improvement in incentives for favorable economic activity. Other supply-side features described in Chapter 3 have had a greater impact on capital investment and other economic activities than have the changes in tax rates.

Tax cuts do, of course, increase aggregate demand, thereby increasing business activity, which in turn stimulates capital investment. But that is not the economic improvement that supply siders emphasize.

Tax rate changes made at the beginning of the Reagan and Clinton administrations were not the *dominant* factors in shaping the economic advances that followed. Other factors were important. What were they? The Reagan administration was faced with the enormous problem of unraveling the economic effects and inflation expectations created by the long inflation cycle that had begun in 1965 and had had a devastating impact on the 1970s. The Federal Reserve could not aggressively stimulate the economy because inflation had not been adequately restrained. The cold war was still at full throttle. Socialism still had its enervating grasp on much of the world. The Clinton administration, by contrast, began with a spectacular array of favorable economic conditions. The long thirty-year inflation cycle was near its end. The Federal Reserve could stimulate the economy substantially without fear of inflation. The cold war was over, allowing substantial reductions in defense spending. Socialism was in its death throes due to the unveiling of its hideous failures in the Soviet Union. The United States had begun a recovery from recession.

Surely the tax rate changes had some impact on incentives, but they were not dominant. Conservatives cannot claim that the 1980s advance was due to improved incentives provided by the tax cut. No one can claim that the 1990s advance was due mainly to the tax increase with its budgetary surplus and irregularly declining long-term interest rates.

Effects of the 2001 to 2003 Tax Cuts

The 2001 tax cut was enacted to stimulate the economy to gain a quick recovery from the recession that had begun early that year. The 2003 tax cut was enacted to bring the quick recovery that the 2001 tax cut had failed to produce. In between, the 2002 tax cut was aimed mainly at giving a temporary boost to capital spending by accelerating depreciation write-offs.

The substantial 2001–3 tax cuts had a *demand*-side stimulative impact on consumer spending. But did they also have a major *supply*-side impact on investment spending? As of this writing in late 2004, little evidence has come to light to demonstrate an important positive impact on investment spending. The rise in the stock market was delayed until 2003 and even then was not unusual. Capital spending by business was also a little slower to recover than after most recessions, as Chart 5.1 shows. Venture capital financing lagged. The huge amount of cash accumulated by business during the 2002–4 period indicated that business had no special incentive to invest in new plant and equipment.

The expressed need for long-term tax-cut incentives to spur investment was perhaps the most startling feature of the justification for the 2001–3 tax cuts. As indicated in Chapter 1, the United States had gone through a half decade of *excessive* capital investment, *excessive* stock market investment, and *excessive* venture capital financing. And yet the 2001–3 tax cuts were promoted on the basis that we needed better incentives to invest than the incentives that had produced *excessive* investment in the last half of the 1990s.

Unless tax disincentives are prohibitive, the best incentive to invest is vigorous consumer spending and an expectation of more to come. That is why a flexible fiscal stimulus plan such as we described in Chapter 1 should be adopted to spur quick recovery from recessions and from periods of slow growth.

Changes in tax rates should, of course, be appraised on grounds in addition to their incentive effects. They must be judged on a basis of fairness as to the burden they place on various groups of taxpayers. They should be judged on the basis of tax efficiencies. How much of the taxes raised is lost due to costs to the government and to the taxpayer? And, of course, as we have already described, the demand-side impact on consumer spending is important.

In Conclusion

A tax system that seriously weakens incentives to work and invest is a heavy burden on any economic system. But to rely on reducing tax disincentives at a time when the *greater* problem is lack of adequate demand or weak structural competition is a grievous error.

Chapter 6

EVOLVING FORCES THAT ARE DRIVING PRODUCTIVITY

Technological improvements are the major long-term drivers of the productivity growth rate. The world has embarked on an accelerating trend of technological change that insures rapid productivity growth for several decades to come. That accelerating technological change is, in turn, being driven by a rapid increase in the number of people engaged in knowledge discovery and invention with ever-increasing amounts of capital equipment at their disposal and driven by increasing competition. We can't possibly know when (if ever), or how, this adventure will end, but it certainly has a long way to run.

Productivity in the United States should improve at an annual rate of 2 1/2 to 3 percent for the next few decades. This is nearly twice the average growth rate of 1 1/2 percent of the 1970s and 1980s. As indicated in Chapter 4, it will double the hourly income of the average worker in about twenty-five years and quadruple it in about fifty years. In many developing countries, productivity will improve much more rapidly as they adopt existing technology. Inventiveness and productivity are now developing on a worldwide basis. This chapter outlines the array of forces driving that development.

GEOGRAPHIC SOURCES OF INCREASED INVENTIVENESS

Countries can be classified into three categories:[5]

1. *Nonmodernizers*. During the 1990s many countries, home to about two billion people (about one-third of the world's population), experienced on average an actual decline in income per head of 1 percent a year. This group included Pakistan, countries of the former Soviet Union, and much of Africa. At the end of the century these countries in the aggregate participated less in international trade than they did twenty years earlier. They failed to attract adequate capital investment and did not properly educate their

children. They were the nonmodernizers. During the 1990s they provided little of the world's inventiveness.

2. *Cheap-labor competitors.* This is the most exciting group of countries because they are going to have such a powerful impact on the world in the twenty-first century. It consists of about twenty-four countries, including China and India, with a total population of about three billion, almost half of the world's population. These twenty-four countries have in the last twenty years integrated into the world's trading community, moving from the production and export of primary products into manufacturing and even services. These countries are the new globalizers. They rely mainly on cheap labor for their competitive advantage. They obtain most of their technology from advanced countries.

These twenty-four countries are still very poor, but poverty has declined substantially. During the 1990s, production grew, in aggregate, about 5 percent, more than twice the growth rate of the rich, advanced countries. That 5 percent growth rate is also five times their 1960s growth rate. These countries achieved their new growth status by improving their investment climate to attract capital investment, providing better education, reducing tariffs, and opening up to foreign investment.

Although these countries rely mainly on cheap labor for their competitive advantage, some of them are now devoting more resources to R&D as companies see the necessity for entering the competition to design new products and processes. Nevertheless, only a small part of the world's inventiveness has so far originated in this large group of countries.

3. *Inventive competitors.* These countries are the rich, advanced countries and are home to just one billion people, about one-sixth of the world's population. They have provided most of the world's inventiveness because firms in these countries have discovered that the invention of new products and processes is the most effective way to compete. They have devoted large resources to education and have allocated the required capital to R&D to become inventive.

Current cheap-labor competitors, home to half the world's population, will provide a gigantic burst of inventiveness throughout the twenty-first century. Their governments generally have recognized the need for attracting capital, both foreign and domestic, in order to modernize. They are learning, often by making mistakes, how to create the necessary economic and political environments to do so. Some of them have increased their R&D spending and in a few categories have already entered the inventive competition arena. As their wage rates rise, their cheap labor advantage diminishes and they are forced to become inventive.

A child recently born will live to see the number of scientists probing nature's secrets at least quadruple. And these scientists will be probing those secrets with instruments hardly dreamed of today. A very large percentage of that huge increase in working scientists will arise as the countries we have designated as cheap-labor competitors turn into inventive competitors. Already China alone is graduating far more scientists and engineers each year than is the United States.

The gradual shift of half the world's population from cheap-labor competition to competition in invention will have other favorable consequences beyond speeding the world's technological development. These countries will have to begin looking abroad for sources of cheap labor rather than being a source of cheap labor themselves. They (and present-day inventive competitors) will have to turn to present-day nonmodernizers for cheap labor. This shift has already begun in a meager way. It will smooth the path of those poverty-stricken, stagnant nonmodernizers toward the more rapid growth now enjoyed by the cheap-labor competitors and move them closer to adding to the world's inventiveness.

Knowledge Discovery as a Chain Reaction

Competition to develop new products is turning knowledge discovery into a chain reaction not unlike the one that takes place in an atomic pile. It will have an explosive impact on productivity. Almost all scientists and inventors give partial credit for their discoveries to an idea, discovery, or invention developed by someone else. That is the very essence of knowledge accumulation. Everyone builds upon the past. If new discoveries stimulate other discoveries, and those discoveries stimulate further discoveries, a chain reaction builds. The energy (new discoveries) released by this chain reaction depends on the number of participants involved and the speed of communication among them. As competition to develop new products and processes spreads around the world, the number of participants in the struggle increases. Communication improves daily. A discovery or invention made anywhere in the world is soon made available to, and benefits, the rest of the world. Indeed, the technological underpinnings of productivity and the New Economy could be explosive.

We will probably one day reach limits to the *rate* of technological change in each industry. Obsolescence may come so fast that firms will delay the adoption of a new technology in the expectation that cost effectiveness would warrant waiting for further improvement. Rising costs of R&D in relation to the commercial value of discoveries may slow development. Only time will tell how soon those limits will be reached in each individual industry. Technological changes will, of course, continue to create new industries in which those limits are far distant.

NEED FOR PEACE AND PROSPERITY

The existence of a large number of capable, competing participants is not enough to guarantee a rapid flow of new inventions. Peace and prosperity are also required. We have attempted to estimate change in the world's inventiveness by examining the number of patents granted by the U.S. Patent Office. Most important inventions made anywhere in the world nowadays result in applications for a patent to the U.S. Patent Office. Consequently, the number of patents granted serves as a rough proxy for the inventiveness of the world.

Chart 6.1 shows the number of patents granted for inventions each year beginning in 1880. Chart 6.2 shows the percentage of total patents that have been granted to foreign individuals, corporations, and governments. Patents granted are not by any means a perfect proxy for R&D spending or inventiveness. All inventions made abroad do not result in patent applications to the U.S. Patent Office. Still, we can make some generalizations about the conditions that encourage inventiveness based on what we see in these two charts.

Chart 6.1 Patents Granted, Inventions Only
U.S. Patent Office

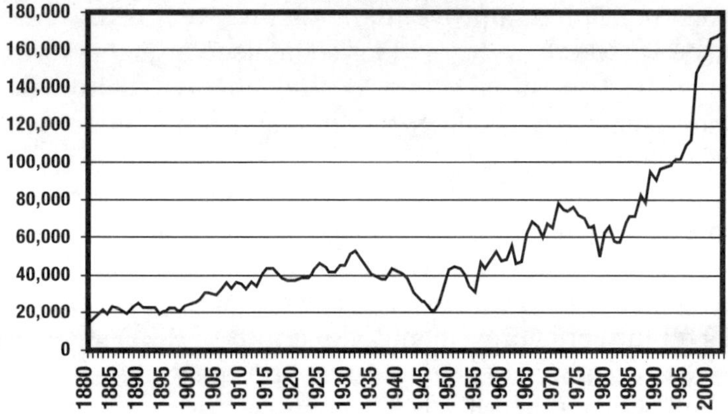

Chart 6.2 Patents Granted to Foreign Individuals, Corporations, and Governments as a Percentage of Total
U.S. Patent Office

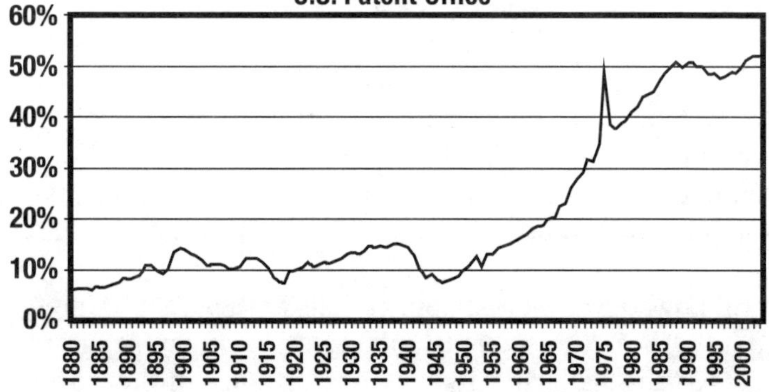

As Chart 6.1 shows, in the mid-1950s the number of patents granted was about the same as the number granted forty years earlier. R&D spending and inventiveness clearly were held back by the wars and the Great Depression. The slump had gone on so long that in the early 1950s a doctoral dissertation and an accompanying article in a professional journal asked whether the rate of invention was declining.[6] But inventiveness soon revived. After World War II, Japan and parts of Europe were in shambles. The recovery of R&D spending and inventiveness was concentrated in the United States, where it continued through the 1960s. The decline of inventiveness in the 1970s as shown on the chart was due to the poor economic performance of the United States with its inflation cycle and recessions. During that period R&D spending in Japan and Europe actually accelerated as they recovered from war devastation. Japan's inventiveness leveled off in the 1990s as it went through a long period of economic stagnation. Clearly, peace and prosperity are basic requirements for R&D spending and inventiveness.

We have argued throughout this little book that the evolving New Economy will continue to improve the management of aggregate demand and structural competition (and therefore the economic environment) in the United States. That improvement will likely also appear throughout most of the world. Furthermore, we will argue in the following chapter that the New Economy will gradually reduce the incidence of war. If that is true, an irregularly improving environment of peace and prosperity will produce a continued rapid growth of invention and productivity. In addition an even more powerful force will improve productivity. In the following chapter we examine the developing competition among governments to attract capital investment. The added impetus of this burgeoning competition will add strength to the growing power of technological change.

Impact of the Improved Organization of Research and Development

The increasing proportion of the world's resources devoted to knowledge discovery and invention is not the only important development. Improved organization of research and development activities has also had a positive impact.

In earlier times, research and development by corporations was done by individual departments within a firm. However, as R&D became more important, specialized research labs were set up to manage that function. Those labs began appearing early in the twentieth century, but they came into their own only after World War II. They have grown to be extremely efficient operations. They can bring together the efforts of scientists from several disciplines and facilitate the exchange of ideas among them. They can establish working relations with other companies including suppliers and customers. They can build financial and professional bridges to universities, government departments, and private research organizations. They can gain feedback from all the departments in their own companies. Perhaps most important, they have the financial clout to delve deeper into the mysteries of nature to pursue long-term goals and thus advance the function of knowledge discovery. We now have a vast network of private companies, universities, governments, and private research organizations that support one another in knowledge discovery and invention on a worldwide basis.[7]

Competition Drives Productivity

So far in this chapter we have described factors that have improved—and will continue to improve—the environment for rapid productivity growth: a rapidly growing number of participants in the inventive process, peace and prosperity, and better organization of the research function. We now add one more—intense competition. Competition has had a powerful impact on productivity. Would productivity in the automobile industry have been nearly as rapid without Japanese and European competition? Would advances in communication have been as spectacular if AT&T had remained the dominant provider? Would computer technology have improved as dramatically if IBM had retained overwhelming domination of the market? Not only must new techniques be invented, but companies must be forced to adopt them. Vigorous competition both drives invention and forces adoption of new technology. The increase in competition on a world-wide basis will help insure a continued rapid improvement in productivity.

Impact of Changes in Management Productivity

So far we have considered the effect of *technological change* on productivity. Technological change is certainly the most important long-term determinant of the productivity growth rate, but changes in *management* productivity are important over short fluctuations in business activity.

What do we mean by changing management productivity? It is the changing productivity most often evidenced by changing competition due to fluctuations in general business activity. In every business there are difficult, risky, and often unpleasant changes that should be made but are postponed simply because they are difficult, risky, or unpleasant. Such changes may include the closing of failed stores, the abandonment of mistaken policies, or the layoff of poorly performing managers.

Inefficiencies due to these postponed decisions build up in periods of rapidly growing business activity. However, when business activity declines, as we go into a recession, competition becomes more intense, firms compete more aggressively for shrinking orders, and workers compete more aggressively for limited jobs. Under increased competition, firms are forced to improve efficiencies to protect profits and sometimes even to survive. In each business downturn, the newspapers are filled with announcements of cost-cutting measures and restructurings. The improvement of the productivity growth rate as business activity declines should not astonish anyone.

Surprisingly, conventional wisdom has it that the productivity growth rate declines as we go into a recession and rises during periods of recovery. But in fact the evidence appears to indicate that the opposite is most often the case.

The bottom line on Chart 6.3 shows the productivity growth rate for nonfinancial corporations over the last half century. The vertical shaded areas mark periods of declining business activity. As the chart shows, the productivity growth rate has begun to *rise* at or near the beginning of each declining phase and has then declined irregularly through most advancing phases. The top line shows capacity utilization in manufacturing. Capacity utilization, of course, declines as business activity declines. That is why we call the increased competition in times of recession *below-capacity competition*. This is the below-capacity competition described in Chapter 3 that the Federal Reserve uses to control inflation when it tightens money, forcing a decline in business activity.

Chart 6.3 Nonfinancial Corporate Productivity Growth Rate and Manufacturing Capacity Utilization, Five-Quarter Moving Average

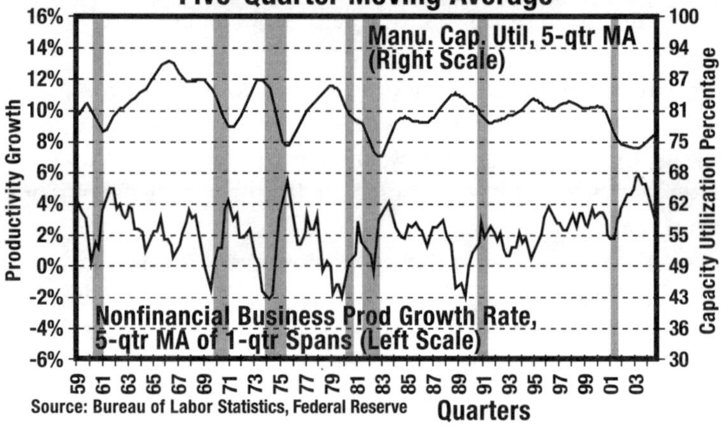

Source: Bureau of Labor Statistics, Federal Reserve

But this improvement in productivity is highly temporary. If a business decline continues for long, most of the management inefficiencies that built up during the period of prosperity will have been corrected. Also, spending on R&D and plant and equipment (that usually embodies new technology) will slow, reducing the rate of technological change. This happened, of course, in the Great Depression.

Changes in management productivity must be examined to understand the changes in the productivity growth rate over periods of expansion and contraction of business activity. This analysis also helps us to understand the importance of competition in keeping productivity growth rates high. Nevertheless, changes in management productivity provide just a minor and temporary exception to our argument that prosperity is necessary for rapid productivity growth.

(The conventional view that the productivity growth rate declines as business activity declines may be partly due to the fact that the growth rate for each month is generally reported as the percent change from the same month in the previous year. This is an *uncentered* moving average and gives a distorted view of the timing of changes in the growth rate relative to the beginning and end of movements in general business activity.)

Chapter 7

THE LONG-TERM WORLD OUTLOOK FOR THE NEW ECONOMY

The long-term world outlook for the New Economy is positively brilliant when compared to the twentieth-century economy with its wars, depressions, inflation, and grinding poverty around much of the world. Changing competition will be the driving force. As described in this chapter, the new competition will be not just among private companies, but increasingly it will be a special kind of competition among governments. It will provide a dynamic environment for the evolution of the New Economy in the United States.

HOW COMPETITION AMONG GOVERNMENTS TO ATTRACT CAPITAL INVESTMENT WILL MOLD THE TWENTY-FIRST CENTURY

For many centuries the course of human events was directed *on a short-term* basis largely by the whims, personal preferences, or religious inclinations of individual heads of authoritarian governments—kings, dictators, commissars, chancellors, ayatollahs, and others. But that is changing. In the tiny speck of time we call the twenty-first century, the course of history will, more and more, be determined by *competition among governments to attract capital investment*. Forces that will drive that competition have already been set in motion by existing bodies of accumulated knowledge. How did it happen?

The envy factor. Most of the people living in developing countries, containing 80 percent of the world's population, envy the people living in advanced countries. They envy the dazzling array of consumer goods, the substantial measure of freedom enjoyed, and the interesting jobs available to qualified workers. Great pressure is put on governments to emulate the success of advanced countries.

How can governments of developing countries modernize to copy the success of the advanced countries? They must obtain vast amounts of capital investment together with necessary technology, management expertise, and markets. But capital investment is in limited supply. Each government must compete with other governments to attract that capital. The winners are those who can provide the most attractive environment for investors. *This competition to provide the best investment environment will largely mold the institutions of the twenty-first century.* Governments in developing countries that we call cheap-labor competitors (including China and India) containing half the world's population have entered the competition with varying degrees of enthusiasm, but all with some degree of success.

How did the advanced countries create the successful political-economic systems that induce such envy and the copying activity that is now under way? These systems are largely the product of three large bodies of accumulated knowledge:

1. *Technology.* The vast body of technical knowledge is an obvious source of the New Economy's abundance. It is what the world sees and what the world wants. But by itself it is not enough.

2. *Competitive markets.* The discovery that the self-serving nature and the often-described "struggle for status" of human beings can be harnessed by the discipline of competitive markets to serve a very large cooperative community involving billions of people has been a spectacular achievement. It is one of the greatest discoveries of all time. In this community, each worker provides a tiny bit of specialized effort and takes out a tiny bit of the total community output. A large body of knowledge has grown up around these markets. It includes ways to manage demand, to protect competition, and to design a money system, as well as solutions to a thousand other problems that arise in competitive markets. This body of knowledge is not fully appreciated by many governments. But sooner or later its general precepts will be learned and to a large extent copied. They must be learned to enable a country to attract the capital investment required to gain necessary technology.

3. *Democratic governance*. Governments, of course, are absolutely necessary. Without them, all would be chaos. They must set and enforce the rules that allow a market economy to work. To keep governmental powers from becoming the playthings of heads of state, a host of techniques have been developed to enable the citizenry to limit those powers. Improving these techniques is still a work in progress. Democratic controls of government are an important part of our body of accumulated knowledge. They will follow, accompany, or sometimes even lead the extension of market competition around the world.

These three bodies of knowledge have created the abundance, freedoms, and opportunities now envied by so many who don't have them. They have, therefore, set in motion the competition to replicate that abundance, freedom, and opportunity. In doing so, they have determined the general outline of human development in the twenty-first century.

Institutional Reforms Spurred by Competition to Attract Capital Investment

One can hardly imagine more favorable circumstances for the design of twenty-first-century institutions than the intense competition to attract capital investment. Most of the things governments must do to win out in the never-ending struggle to modernize are well known. They include at least five categories.

1. Governments must provide a workable, generally accepted rule of law (including an independent judiciary) to protect private property and the primacy of contract. This is essential to attract necessary capital investment from abroad but is also important for attracting capital investment from within a country. Hernando DeSoto of Peru has written a fascinating book, *The Mystery of Capital*, in which he describes how enormous amounts of capital investment could be created by improving the law governing property rights in several poor developing countries.[8] Many farmers, proprietors of small businesses, and home occupants control property only by dint of possession. Property is not officially recognized by deed or other instruments providing legal protec-

tion. Therefore, this property cannot easily be used for collateral on which to borrow funds for expansion, including the creation of new capital. It cannot easily be sold to gain funds for capital investment in other ventures. DeSoto calls these assets dead capital that could be activated by giving them the documented legal status already provided to property owned by large enterprises.

2. An environment of peace and tolerance is needed to allow buyers and sellers, investors and entrepreneurs, teachers and students to move safely and comfortably around the country, and indeed around the world. Tourism especially requires tolerance, and tourism has become a major source of funds that developing countries can use to acquire capital equipment. Not surprisingly, intolerant Iran has languished near the bottom of the list of countries ranked by foreign tourist income as a percentage of GDP.

3. Governments must maintain considerable fiscal responsibility, avoiding unnecessary spending, taxation, and borrowing. Appropriate bank regulation is an important part of this fiscal responsibility. Failure in the fiscal arena shows up as inflation, lost incentives, excessive budget deficits, widening current account deficits, bank failures, and eventually unemployment and stagnation. Bond, stock, and currency markets nowadays levy severe penalties on governments for lax fiscal policies, discouraging capital investment in the process.

4. Besides providing an appropriate legal and fiscal framework, a government must provide a decent human environment in order to attract the best capital investment. Of course, citizens must be properly educated and trained. This is especially true when a country graduates from its initial comparative advantage of providing cheap labor and moves into the competition for designing, selling, and maintaining sophisticated products.

5. Corruption must be minimized. Transparency International, a nongovernmental organization, conducts periodic surveys to estimate the prevalence of corruption in various countries. Clearly, the most corrupt countries attract the least direct foreign investment. Corruption is most prevalent when government regulation is extensive, providing an

army of regulators with the power to extract bribes in return for favorable decisions. Ration coupons, housing permits, travel authorizations, business licenses, job opportunities—these are examples of the authorizations that government employees can trade for bribes in countries where governments maintain extensive control of an economy. Minimizing corruption generally requires a shrinking of government regulation of economic activity.

Industrialized countries, as well as developing countries, are faced with this competition to attract capital investment. The competitive pressure to improve the investment climate never ends. Governments of industrialized countries are under pressure to continue making all those improvements that developing countries must make to attract capital investment. When they fail to do so, they see their own firms channel investments to friendlier environments, and they attract little offsetting investment from abroad.

Competition among governments to attract capital investment, of course, has limitations. Obviously, it will not *necessarily* solve problems where solutions require international agreements among competing countries, and where solutions *initially* appear to harm some countries. Global warming may turn out to be a case in point. Yet, international cooperation among competing governments has already racked up some notable achievements. The development of institutions to facilitate international trade is a magnificent accomplishment. International police cooperation is another. There will likely be many more.

Of course, no country has to make all those above-listed reforms before it can begin to attract capital investment. But some progress must be made and a trend toward an investment-friendly environment must be evident. Sooner or later, an investment-friendly government will arise in all countries as the pressure to modernize becomes irresistible. Countries simply cannot go far toward modernization without becoming part of the international investment community. Unfortunately, in a number of countries, such a government will arise later rather than sooner. Nevertheless, movement toward reform is unmistakable.

Although we argue strongly that the responsibility for the economic improvement of developing countries lies mainly with those countries, nothing in this book should be construed to imply that that development could not be moderately speeded by intelligent foreign aid from advanced countries or by greater opening of advanced-country markets.

Determinism?

The strong predictions we have made about the twenty-first century sound highly deterministic, as though people have no choice as to what will happen. That's far from the truth. We are simply arguing that the great majority of the world's population has *already* chosen modernization, and that that choice will determine much of twenty-first-century development. The remaining choices involve how to get there, and in these choices people have considerable latitude. Yet, the coming choice of government policies will surely be constrained by the need to attract capital and the need to educate populations, both of which will require the policies previously outlined.

Furthermore, people will gain far greater power than they have ever had before to choose where they work, what goods and services they consume, and what kind of government they live under. Through their demand in the marketplace, they will order producers to provide the goods they want. Through democratic processes, they will have considerable power (constrained by preferences of other voters) to control the government policies under which they live. Indeed, the choice of modernization will eventually deliver an enormous range of meaningful choice to people *because* government policy will be constrained by the requirements to attract capital investment and provide adequate educational opportunities.

Impediments to Modernization

The pressures to modernize to achieve the freedoms, the attractive job opportunities, and the wealth of market-managed economies are powerful, but so also are the well-known impediments. Those impediments include many authoritarian governments, entrenched bureaucrats, monopolists in both labor and product markets, and others who are *initially* hurt by a turn to a competitive economy. Impediments of a social nature include ideas, habits, customs, religious convictions, and embedded hatreds that are difficult to dislodge. But many countries are overcoming these obstacles and are building the investment-friendly environments necessary to modernize. They are setting performance standards by which other governments are judged. The necessity to attract capital will intrude upon most decisions each government makes. Decisions will often be painful. Governments will have to compromise cherished traditions and temporarily alienate some of their people. The pressure to do so will be great.

Myriad forces are constantly interacting with one another to determine the events of the day and to change (or prevent the change of) institutions that will direct the events of the future. Some of these forces are strong. Others are weak. The strong forces are *controlling* forces. The weak forces are *adaptive* forces. When adaptive forces come up against a controlling force, they must give way to that stronger power. We have projected that the need to modernize, working mainly through competition to attract capital investment, will be by far the strongest of the forces controlling governments throughout most of the twenty-first century. It will be so powerful that it will eventually override those impediments to peace and prosperity that now seem so intractable but in the end will prove to be just weak adaptive forces. It will overcome opposing ideas and customs, as well as embedded hatreds.

There is no *realistic* alternative to modernization by attracting capital investment. The alternatives so far chosen by some governments (or by the people they are trying to govern) would, if continued, keep their countries in poverty, intermittent military conflict, and hopelessness while they watch a large and growing share of the world move rapidly onto the road toward modernization with its wealth, freedoms, and opportunities. Those alternatives to modernization by attracting capital investment are not realistic. They will eventually be abandoned. If the forces driving modernization are so powerful, does the nature of existing governments really matter? Of course it does. The wisdom, or lack of wisdom, of present-day leaders will determine how long and how painful the transition to New Economy conditions will be.

Many present-day nonmodernizing countries are caught in a Malthusian trap. Rapidly growing populations are pressing against relatively fixed production capabilities. Standards of living are declining. The only way to break out of this trap is to enter the competition to attract capital investment. To do that, countries must move toward those features necessary to attract capital investment as described earlier in this chapter. That will not be easy. Countries such as Iran, whose leadership is staunchly resisting significant change, are inviting an eventual sudden change in leadership. If delayed for long, such change could be violent.

Although impediments to modernization often seem unyielding, we are entitled to look beyond the prevalence of entrenched hatreds and misconceptions, beyond the prevalence of unscrupulous and self-serving governments, and focus on the many places in the world where competition among private producers and competition among governments are making great progress.

By-Products of Competition to Attract Capital Investment

By-products of the competition to attract capital investment are substantial. Billions of people will move from farms to factories, stores, and offices in urban environments. Their fertility rates will decline, bringing the world's population growth rate down to zero probably not long after the middle of the twenty-first century. Pressure on the world's space will moderate. Funds (and incentives) to protect the environment will become available as modernization brings a moderate degree of affluence.

Our forecast that the output of most developing countries will match the output of advanced countries, which will, in turn, continue to grow rapidly, will give many environmentalists nightmares. Actually, it is the best outcome that environmentalists can reasonably hope for because it is the quickest (only?) way to bring population growth under control. The possibility that developing countries will delay industrialization until their populations have doubled and *then* industrialize should make for far worse nightmares. Rapid industrialization is important.

From Malthus to the present, forecasts of imminent disaster due to limitations of resources have been upset by improving technology. If our analysis in Chapter 6 is correct that the world has embarked on an accelerating rate of knowledge discovery and invention, improving technology should solve problems due to population growth during the period while it is still expanding.

More effective democracy will be another by-product of the competition among governments to attract capital investment. Democracy is not a *prerequisite* for the establishment of competitive markets. In fact, one might argue that the many dislocations, lost privileges, and unequal opportunities that arise in the change from a government-managed economy to an economy managed by competitive markets can best be handled initially by an authoritarian government as long as that government is seriously dedicated to reform.

Though not a prerequisite, substantial democracy will be a by-product of the establishment of competitive markets. A turn away from extensive government management always results in a shrinkage of the power and presence of government. When citizens no longer face government factotums who have great discretion to say yes or no, at the school, store, housing authority, license bureau, ration agency, employment office, and other places, their fear of government diminishes, and they begin demanding more civil and political liberties. The ability of government to track and discipline people wanes. Democratic procedures eventually follow.

Finally, how will competition to attract capital affect the distribution of the world's rapidly growing wealth and income, both among countries and among individuals? The output of present-day cheap-labor-competitive countries containing half the world's population has been growing much faster percentagewise than the output of advanced countries. As their wage rates rise, they will have to turn toward the present-day poverty-stricken, nonmodernizing countries for cheap labor. That will gradually bring those countries into the group that is gaining on the advanced countries. The gap between rich and poor countries will be dramatically narrowed during the twenty-first century.

As for income distribution among individuals, right now there are billions of poorly paid, unskilled (or lightly skilled) workers in the world. They include less-talented people and many naturally talented people who never had the opportunity to get the education and training required to command better-paying jobs, even if such jobs were available. But cheap-labor-competitive countries are being forced by competition to provide better education and training and will gradually attract the capital investment that will provide better jobs. Therefore, as the twenty-first century develops, there will be far fewer unskilled workers in the world competing for the same jobs. Fast-forward five or ten decades. Who in the United States will do the drudge work on farms or in cities when there are few immigrants or guest workers to do that work? Who will do the repetitive work in factories when cheap goods can no longer be imported in huge quantities manufactured by cheap labor in developing countries? The less-talented will be doing the drudge work both on farms and in cities, but with far fewer extremely low-paid unskilled workers around the world to compete with, the less-talented workers in the United States will command much better relative pay.

The Changing Nature of Competition Among Governments

Few will deny that a vicious competition among governments has prevailed during most of recorded history. Much of the rivalry was driven by the desire to achieve wealth, power, and prestige for the governments themselves and for the countries they ruled. Often, the desired power was to extend religious domination. The acquisition of land and its natural resources, together with the people who worked the land, was the primary method of adding to wealth, power, and prestige. But the supply of land is relatively fixed. To add to territorial holdings meant seizing land from some other government. And that usually meant war, the main expression of intergovernmental competition throughout most of recorded history.

Rivalry among governments still prevails and is still being driven largely by the desire to achieve wealth, power, and prestige. The big difference is that the technique for achieving those goals has changed dramatically. Whereas the control of land and the people working the land was once the measure of success, nowadays the quantity and quality of productive capital is becoming the critical measure. Adding to land meant taking it from another government, usually resulting in war. Adding to productive capital more often results in cooperation of governments through international trade and through the functioning of the international investment community, even though considerable bickering arises at the many points where competitors meet. Surely the ability of governments to satisfy the drive for wealth, power, and prestige without resort to war is one of the most valuable gifts of modern technology. As more governments become aware of the necessity to make their countries attractive places for capital investment to achieve those long-standing goals of wealth, power and prestige, the New Economy should provide a more peaceful era in which to live.

The Problem-Solving Capability of the New Economy

Might some presently unforeseen event arise that will seriously delay the worldwide extension of the New Economy? Of course it might. If some currently unexpected problem comes along equivalent in seriousness to the twentieth century's Great Depression, will the New Economy be able to solve it? Or will competitive capitalism suffer another long setback like the twentieth century swing to socialism, which was in large part due to the perceived failure of capitalism produced by the Great Depression?

What determines problem-solving capability? *The existence of a large number of capable participants with an opportunity to innovate and under competitive pressure to do so provides the best environment for problem solving.* As competitive market economies spread around the world, these conditions will expand in the private production sector, guaranteeing a widening flow of new, better, and less expensive products and services to solve long-standing problems such as human disease, as well as to satisfy wants that the New Economy will generate. But the more exciting prospect is the new competition among governments.

When the Great Depression struck, there was just a handful of reasonably well-established capitalist countries. Furthermore, most of the economists in those countries had learned their economics out of the same textbooks. Consequently, few innovative approaches to solving the problem were devised until the depression had done great damage. But now there are many reasonably well-established capitalist countries, each one trying to find a superior solution to current problems. We have moved a long way toward the environment of having many reasonably capable government participants with opportunities to innovate and under competitive pressure to do so. Every act of governance now must face critical comparison to its counterparts designed by competing governments in many other jurisdictions. The most successful ones are eventually copied. The chance of solving the problems generated by the New Economy are improving as the number of capitalist governments increases, each trying to outperform the others. For example, look at the variety of approaches for dealing with fluctuating foreign exchange rates. They have varied from free-floating rates to fixed rates. Recent experience appears to indicate that relatively free-floating rates are better, except perhaps in very special circumstances. History has demonstrated that fixed exchange rates are frequently disastrous. They have largely been abandoned. This type of experimentation among competing governments will be the wave of the future. It should vastly improve the problem-solving capability of New Economy governments.

Optimism Based on Governments' Problem-Solving Capabilities

No forecast of the economic and political outlook for the United States and the world more optimistic than the ones we have made in this book is anywhere likely to be found. What do we see that pessimistic forecasters do not? *Surprisingly, we have greater confidence in the ability of governments to solve problems.* To repeat, the best conditions for problem solving exist when many participants have the freedom to innovate and are under competitive pressure to do so. All three of the conditions in that statement have improved dramatically in recent years—freedom to innovate, a large number of participants involved, and action driven by competition.

1. *Freedom to innovate.* For most of the half century since World War II, the problem-solving ability of many governments was under the constraints of the cold war and socialist dogma. Governments dictated policy and allowed little experimentation. But those constraints were shattered just a little more than a decade ago with the fall of the Berlin Wall leading to the collapse of the Soviet Union. The disclosure of the abysmal performance of the Soviet economy—that paragon of socialism—dealt a near-fatal blow to the already wilting socialist dogma that had shackled policy making in many countries for decades. The end of the cold war also freed many governments whose policies had been chained to the requirements of the particular cold war camp to which they were tied. A new sense of freedom to try innovative approaches appeared. A new sense of dynamism arose. The world is now changing at a faster pace, bringing new problems related to the transition to new policies. Governments have far greater opportunity (and pressure) to innovate than they had under socialist dogma and the cold war. We wonder how many people fully appreciate the significance to government of this recent outbreak of freedom, innovation, and change.

2. *Large number of participants.* Far more governments are now involved in designing market-managed economies than ever before. The majority of governments have accepted the need to modernize and have recognized (often tentatively) the need to make some change toward a market-managed economy. Each government faces its own particular set of circumstances and problems, so each government has to design a slightly (or vastly) different approach to development. Innovation is essential. Yet, with so many countries involved, each government has examples, some good, some bad, in each stage of development to look to for suggestions. There are now many varieties of competitive-market economies. There will be more. They arise as many participants experiment with new approaches to solving problems.

3. *Competitive pressure to perform.* Governments face serious rivalries in their race to gain wealth, power, and prestige. As described earlier, intergovernmental rivalry nowadays plays out more in the economic and social spheres than in the military sphere as it once did when wealth, power, and prestige were usually gained by taking territory from some other government. But that rivalry among governments is still very real and, we believe, will force governments to take painful steps to solve their problems. For example, proud Germany for the past few years has had to bear the stigma of being an economic laggard, dragging down the economy of the Euro zone. To catch up with its neighbors, it is now taking very painful steps to weaken the monopolistic power of its labor unions in order to improve the competitive discipline of its markets. Japan, after a decade of stagnation, is finally taking painful steps to get its banking system back in order. Competitive pressure from rapidly growing South Korea, Taiwan, and others may be a factor. China sets a competitive pace for India. A few countries such as Zimbabwe and Venezuela are at the moment going the wrong way, but hardly a week goes by without some country announcing an improvement in its management of the environment for a competitive market. Competition among governments is strong. Its power to force governments to solve their problems should not be underestimated. Competition to attract

capital investment will put unrelenting pressure on governments to perform.

Of course, the very nature of government problem solving precludes the kind of excellent performance we would like to see. Government decisions in democracies are always a product of compromises (often defective ones) between competing interests. Compromises are usually slow in coming, sometimes dreadfully slow. Nevertheless, government decision making should be far better than in the Very Old Economy of the first half of the twentieth century or the Old Economy of the second half of that century.

RELAPSE?

Prior to World War I the world basked in a sense of optimism. Trade was expanding. The world had been relatively peaceful for decades. Productivity was surging with rising standards of living. The future looked bright. Then came the war, ushering in hyperinflation, the Great Depression, Hitler, World War II, socialism, and the cold war. Most historians quite properly consider the possibility of a similar relapse in the twenty-first century. But it's not likely.

The capitalism of that earlier time was primitive. The few countries that professed to be capitalist were ignorant of some of the basic requirements of successful capitalism. They did not understand how to design workable money and banking systems, or how to manage aggregate demand, or how to maintain adequate structural competition. Furthermore, that primitive capitalism had not had enough time to produce the rule of law, the civil liberties, and the democratic governments necessary to maintain peaceful, prosperous societies.

As other chapters have described, we have learned much about managing a capitalist economy. Most of that learning has been done the hard way, by making mistakes and then recognizing the reasons why the mistaken policies didn't work. We will continue to make mistakes, but the basic framework of a workable capitalist system has been established. Mistakes will most likely be made at the periphery and will do less damage than some of the mistakes of the past.

We will not have to wait centuries for present-day developing countries to join present-day advanced countries in the group of reasonably successful capitalist democracies. Since the collapse of the Soviet Union with its vivid exposure of socialist failures and with its end to the cold war, the transition has gained phenomenal speed. Within fifty years, at least half the five-sixths of the world's population now in the developing stage will likely be living in reasonably effective capitalist democracies. Most of the other half should follow in the succeeding fifty years.

China, with one-fifth of the world's population, is wonderfully suited to make the transition. First, it has an authoritarian government that can keep order through those arduous adjustments to the new system. South Korea, Taiwan, Singapore, and Chile were similarly situated as they made the transition. Democracies seldom make the adjustment quickly, if at all. Second, *and more important*, China's government is apparently aware of the need to provide an environment suitable to attract capital investment, both domestic and foreign, to achieve their desperately desired modernization. Furthermore, China's government has the memory of a failed attempt to retrogress away from the shift to a market-managed economy. After the shock of the Tiananmen Square incident in 1989, China's government made an effort to reassert control by moving back toward greater government management. Waves of bankruptcies followed. The economy stagnated. The shift to capitalism was quickly restarted. Capitalism was able to survive because it had proved that it works. And it was only a single-decade-old rudimentary capitalism that had performed so much better than the earlier socialist system. As capitalism develops, civil liberties and democracy will follow.

India, with one-sixth of the world's population, has more serious problems. For more than forty years after independence in 1947, India was shackled by very bad economic ideas. It was socialist. It was dedicated to national self-sufficiency and cut itself off from international trade and investment as much as possible. India was also devoted to simple, small-scale production units and thus was late in seeking modern technology. It was a democracy with widely disparate religious, caste, language, and other ethnic groups that could not easily cooperate to change the failing system. Not until the Soviet collapse with its socialist embarrassments and the success of Chinese competitors were significant movements to capitalism undertaken. Efforts have continued sporadically. Considerable economic-management authority has shifted to the states. Competition among these states and with the economic giant to the north appear to be the spur necessary to keep the transition continuing. It seems unlikely that even India's squabbling democracy will stand by and allow China to move further and further ahead. Competition to modernize is a powerful force.

Russia is an important country, not because of the size of its population, but because it holds all those nuclear-tipped ICBMs. Russia attempted to move to democracy shortly after the breakup of the Soviet Union. The effort proved disastrous. Russia had horrendous problems. It had no law governing private productive property. It had no middle class. It had no tradition of civil liberties. Democracy collapsed quickly, and although elections are still held, the government has become strongly authoritarian. But like China, its government appears dedicated to shift to substantial market management of the economy. Competition with its neighbors (and the rest of the world) should keep it on that path. No other system could achieve the necessary modernization. The outlook for Russia to make a favorable transition to a capitalist economy is reasonably good. Genuine democracy will follow.

Arab countries, and by extension the entire Muslim community making up about one-fifth of the world's population, are of headline importance at the moment. What are the prospects for a prompt and successful transition to capitalist democracies? Prospects are grim but not hopeless.

Part of the Muslim community is experiencing a religious revival led by vocal groups that are generally known as Islamic fundamentalists. These fundamentalists propose the establishment of societies governed by an extreme interpretation of Islamic law (Sharia) similar to those that prevailed under the Taliban in Afghanistan and have existed in Iran since the overthrow of the Shah twenty-five years ago. Fundamentalists are opposed to Western-style modernization, and so competition to attract capital investment in order to modernize is not a driving force. That is, not yet. But it may not be far away. For twenty-five years Iran's economy has been deteriorating under the kind of government-managed Islamic economy proposed by the fundamentalists. It will continue to deteriorate. Iran's population is growing rapidly. A large proportion is under the age of 25. A breakdown may come soon. That bad example, plus the already-revealed failures of the Taliban in Afghanistan may turn Muslims toward modernization by attracting capital investment.

On the other side, examples of Muslim countries that are modernizing successfully by attracting capital investment are proliferating. Turkey, Malaysia, Morocco, Tunisia, and Jordan are moving slowly along that road. They will likely provide improving positive examples of successful societies that maintain the essentials of the Muslim faith while modernizing. Iraq, post-Saddam, could turn out to be another positive example.

But ultimately the establishment of a *viable* independent Palestinian state will be necessary to turn Muslims away from militancy toward efforts to attract capital investment. That, plus a successful rebuilding of Iraq along capitalist (and Muslim) lines would likely provide a reasonably prompt and dramatic launch for a major development of the entire region and even the entire Muslim community. So much is at stake.

In Conclusion

Recent decades have marked the fading away of a very bad and widespread idea—socialism. These same decades (as described in Chapter 3) have marked major improvements in understanding how to manage a capitalist system. Those developments in knowledge accumulation together with the burgeoning competition among governments to attract capital investment provide an optimistic tint to the twenty-first century outlook.

Chapter 8

OPTIMISM—VALID OR NOT?

Overoptimism is deadly. Valid optimism is necessary to keep the struggle alive. Is our optimism valid? If it is, why do so many people believe that the world is falling apart? One answer is obvious. The weakening of many authoritarian governments has allowed the release of many bottled-up hatreds, desires, and fears that have been suppressed for decades (centuries?) by those authoritarian governments. Some of these outbursts are violent. In the transition to the New Economy, the world seems somewhat more chaotic than before. But there is a more fundamental reason—the culture wars that are being intensified by the shift to the New Economy.

CULTURE WARS IN THE NEW ECONOMY

Culture wars are a raucous feature of New Economy societies. What are they? Every society must have devices to manage human behavior in order to stay functional. Management devices include formal laws and regulations together with informal customs, traditions, and manners. *Culture wars are conflicts over behavior patterns and the nature of those management devices.* In the United States, conflict is waged over issues such as these that have been linked to the culture wars on the Internet and elsewhere: abortion, gay rights, morality, struggle to define America, religion, political correctness, violence in movies, prostitution, drugs, affirmative action, feminism, crime deterrence, freedom of speech, and penal policy.

The New Economy intensifies culture wars in several ways:

• *Rapid technological change* requires continued adjustments to behavior patterns, upsetting established traditions. For example, modern technology has brought a large proportion of women into the labor force, thereby impacting most aspects of family life and relations between men and women.

The conflicts sparked by various ramifications of sex and gender are part of our daily news.

• *Spread of democracy* and its accompanying behavioral freedoms often make for increased cultural conflict. People living under authoritarian regimes that lay down rigid rules of conduct simply do not have the power to change behavioral patterns. Widespread debate is generally useless if not prohibited. Culture wars are less pervasive.

• *Increasing discretionary income* expands opportunity to engage in a much wider range of activities, increasing the diversity of human behavior and the diversity of interests that generate conflict.

• *Globalization* throws incompatible cultures more and more into contact with one another, setting the stage for increased *cultural* conflict.

Which cultural traits will survive the culture wars? Modern technology has decreed that we must live and work together in large groups with complex interrelationships. The ability to live and work together without disruptive conflict is, therefore, one of the most precious characteristics any society can possess. *Countries that protect and promote those cultural traits that facilitate efficient and harmonious interrelationships will have a distinct advantage* in the new world of nonmilitary competition among countries, governments, and cultures.

As competition among governments to attract capital investment spreads market-managed economic conditions around the world, *economic* performance among laggard countries will gradually catch up with that of the more advanced countries. There will still be differences, but they will be far smaller than they are now. We suggest that a world dominated by fairly similar economic performances will find that the ability to achieve harmonious interrelationships will be the major factor denoting prestige on the world stage. For example, countries that have to keep a substantial portion of their populations in prison or have a welfare program that produces a large proportion of malingerers will rank low on the prestige scale.

Countries will have many opportunities to improve the

relationships that the organizations and activities of the New Economy demand. Irregularly advancing New Economy conditions will provide the funding, incentives, and knowledge necessary to improve our ability to devise better formal and informal ways to manage human behavior patterns. Surely expanded research and experimentation should be able to come up with far superior answers to managing mundane aspects of human behavior such as drug addiction.

Which cultural traits will fail? No cultural trait clearly incompatible with modernization or with the forces we have described that are making modernization possible will survive unchanged. Some will survive for a while, but those that seriously impede the attraction of capital investment or the expansion of education are doomed to ultimate failure.

Culture wars will be a continuing, probably intensifying, aspect of the New Economy. Nevertheless, the capital-attraction requirement of modernization will keep most culture wars from escalating into real war. Peace is necessary to attract capital investment. The area of stability in the world is gradually expanding, and the area of instability is gradually shrinking.

Views of Human Nature

When it comes to the culture wars, we cannot argue as confidently that optimism is justified. One's degree of optimism or pessimism will depend on one's view of human nature. The New Economy is delivering to the world choices in the marketplace and in the voting booth that would have seemed unimaginable to most of the world's inhabitants only a few decades ago. Will these freedoms to choose be used wisely or badly? Some people believe that we humans are essentially depraved. We will choose sloth and debauchery and end up in a modern Sodom and Gomorrah. Others believe that our depravity will lead us to vote for governments that will sacrifice compassion for the weak to allow the highly talented and ruthless to take the lion's share of our wealth while the less talented languish in poverty and hopelessness. Still others believe that we will vote for more and more government largess that will destroy incentives, leading to collapse of our economic system. Fear of "irrational" religious beliefs that lead to perpetual conflict worries others. Any of these views and thousands of others may be held in moderation or in extremity, or in combination with one another. They mold our views of the future, optimistic or pessimistic. We have made confident projections about the world's economic performance. But our optimistic view of the outcome of the culture wars is less confident. Through product, labor, and financial markets and through the ballot box the masses are taking command. Who can say, with certainty, where their nature (whatever it is) will take us? Religious teachers, philosophers, and curious, reflective individuals have been arguing about the nature of man for millennia with little discernible agreement.

Forecasting Is Getting a Bit Easier

We have made a number of confident predictions about coming developments of the New Economy. Is such confidence warranted?

As indicated earlier, throughout most of history, events of the day were determined mainly by the personal interests, desires, religious inclinations, even whims of powerful heads of government—kings, dictators, chancellors, commissars, ayatollahs, and others. While technological developments were slowly grinding out the long-term destiny of the human race, these powerful heads of state were determining the short-term course of history. To forecast short-term and medium-term developments required forecasting the personal proclivities of a few powerful, often unpredictable people.

Times are changing. Accumulated human knowledge has created market-managed economies and democratic governments that have delivered great power into the hands of the people. Investors control many aspects of government simply by their choice of investments.

Workers influence government by where they choose to live and work. Consumers control both business and government by their choices in buying (or not buying). And voters, of course, have massive influence on government through the ballot box. All in all, much power has been transferred from heads of state to the public. This makes forecasting a bit easier. For example, voting populations will usually turn out of office any administration that allows serious economic stagnation and high unemployment to persist. That fact allows us to make useful predictions as to how governments will behave to avoid being turned out of office. At least making such predictions is easier than trying to divine the whims of kings.

Identifying Controlling Forces

We attempt to forecast by identifying and evaluating forces that will direct human behavior. This is true whether we are trying to forecast the S&P 500 stock average or the long-term population growth rate. In Chapter 7 we attempted to demonstrate that the need to modernize will produce a powerful competition among governments to create the best environment to attract capital investment and that that competition will bring some remarkably favorable developments to the world. We believe that the competition to attract capital investment will be by far the dominant force in molding the institutions of the twenty-first century.

We have described some other forces that will direct events of the coming decades. The aging of the population and the growing complexity of society will produce unrelenting pressure to increase social services. The increasing *variety* of products flowing from New Economy industry will require ever-widening trading areas to find the specialists required to produce those goods efficiently.

But the accumulating body of human knowledge and its counterpart, the fading away of bad ideas, is the most fundamental of all forces we have considered. We suggest that it has been the *long-term* designer of human institutions throughout history. The innate intelligence, curiosity, and inventiveness of human beings have kept that body of knowledge growing.

The Accumulation of Human Knowledge

We cannot resist the temptation to look briefly at the entire sweep of history to see if the accumulation of human knowledge can usefully be considered as the basic controlling force that has directed long-term human developments and will continue to do so. We divide accumulated knowledge into two parts—technological and organizational. The pool of technological knowledge is easily identified. It includes all those discoveries and inventions from before the wheel to after the transistor. The pool of organizational knowledge is more fascinating and challenging. It includes an understanding of all those aspects of human society that affect relations among people. Families, tribes, religions, customs, traditions, laws, courts, governments, and so on are the institutions that dominate that pool of organizational knowledge.

Developments Over Thousands of Years

Intelligent, curious, inventive human beings have been grinding out new products and better ways of producing them for millennia. The pool of *technological* knowledge has, over those thousands of years, grown inexorably, although for a long time slowly. Lately it has grown at astonishing speed. The pool of *organizational* knowledge, describing how people live and work together, has grown more slowly with more setbacks and with less assurance of success. For several millennia, authoritarian governments and religions were the dominant *large-scale* players active in the pool of organizational knowledge. But gradually a third player—the market—intruded into the organizational space.

It began with the appearance of specialists. Those people who could produce one product better than other people could, produced more than they needed. They traded part of their output for products produced by superior producers of other goods. As technologies increased the *variety* of goods, specialists proliferated and something happened—the market came into being. Pockets of traders arose along sea coasts, rivers, and land routes. Markets were not deliberately designed. They appeared naturally to fill the need for trade among specialists. As the variety of goods expanded due to that growing pool of technological knowledge, markets widened due to what we have called in Chapter 3 the Geographic Law of Specialization: *the greater the variety of goods produced, the wider the trading area necessary to find the specialists to produce those goods*. The efficiencies of markets improved. Banks arose to facilitate financing. Laws developed to facilitate necessary contractual relations. The growing pool of technological knowledge improved transportation and communication.

The Last Few Centuries

In the pool of organizational knowledge, authoritarian governments began to feel a few pinpricks from democratic ideology. But those authoritarian governments gave up little power. Finally, however, a major new force entered that pool of organizational knowledge. Adam Smith and others recognized that the competitive market could be an extremely effective organizational device to channel the troublesome self-interest inherent in most people into a dynamic effort to serve a worldwide cooperative community. Capitalism entered the pool of organizational knowledge. It was not fully formed nor understood. But it survived because it worked, not beautifully but far better than the alternative: government management of trade among specialists.

Over the last few centuries the pool of organizational knowledge has been dominated by the interplay of authoritarian governments, religions, competitive markets (capitalism), and the upstart spirit of democratic yearnings. We recommend Chapter 1 of Fareed Zakaria's book *The Future of Freedom* as a guide to the intricate interactions of these protagonists of organizational knowledge over the past few centuries.[9] He quite properly emphasizes the need for freedom, especially economic freedom, *to precede* democracy if that democracy is to be effective and survive. He also describes how the breakup of religious hierarchies and authoritarian governments made possible the rise of market-oriented institutions.

Organizational Knowledge and the Rise of the New Economy

In just the last two decades, competitive market principles (capitalism) have taken command of the pool of organizational knowledge. Those capitalist principles have become much more effective as countries have improved their management of aggregate demand and structural competition to provide a better environment in which markets can flourish, as described in Chapter 3. The primary economic antagonist—socialist ideology—is in full retreat due to its many failures recently unveiled.

Competition among governments to modernize by attracting capital investment is gradually but inexorably forcing governments to adopt policies that will establish competitive markets. Civil liberties and genuine democracy will follow. Authoritarian governments will continue to put up a powerful rearguard action, but their days are numbered.

That will leave religion as the sole survivor of the large-scale players that dominated the pool of organizational knowledge for millennia. What is the New Economy doing to religion? The capital investment requirement of the New Economy requires peace and tolerance. This will gradually end the militancy of most religious zealots and will reduce the dictating of harsh behavioral codes by religion-dominated governments.

The worldwide trade and migration brought about by the New Economy need for wide markets will, over a long period, bring *competition* to religion as people find that under New Economy tolerance they can choose among various faiths with which they come in contact. That should improve the performance of various religions. It is not a coincidence that the United States has the most active religious community among historically Christian countries. Competition among religions in the United States has existed from almost the beginning. That competition has forced religious establishments to better serve the needs of their members. It will take a long time, but competition among religions, intensified by worldwide trade and migration, should vastly improve the nature of the world's faiths.

Religion will survive and flourish in modified form and stand along with competitive market economies and democracies as a large-scale player in the pool of organizational knowledge. Everyone needs a sense of belonging, preferably to a group with similar beliefs and aspirations. Religions can provide that sense of belonging. They will also fill the important functions of giving hope and comfort. And they will continue the critical function of teaching the rules by which people can live and work together in harmony.

In Conclusion

To repeat, every glint of optimism expressed throughout this little book is based on faith in the learning process: in our appraisal of what we have learned, the speed with which we are learning, and *the competitive forces that are driving us to continue to learn.* Both people and governments have learned and are continuing to learn at accelerating speed. *Much of the pessimism so frequently expressed in the media appears to be based on the conviction that people and governments will not learn.* Yes, overoptimism is deadly. But valid optimism is necessary to keep the struggle alive. Counsels of despair should be avoided. The wind is at our backs.

Can anyone read the history of the American twentieth century and *not* conclude that we have learned an immense amount that has improved the management of the market economy? And is there anything in that history to lead us to believe that that learning process is now at an end? Can we not learn to reduce even further our recent historically mild employment shortfall? Can we not learn how to better manage the social-service side of a competitive market economy? Can we not delight in the competition among governments to attract capital investment that is forcing them to continue to learn?

Change will not come easily. But it will come as we solve those problems left behind by the bad ideas that have hampered the world's development for centuries. Knowledge is power.

Appendix

INVESTMENT POLICIES FOR THE NEW ECONOMY

This appendix provides an example of the practical uses of New Economy analysis. It was not prepared by Crossroads Research Institute (Crossroads is involved with stock market analysis only to the extent that the market impacts the economy.) but rather by investors who use New Economy principles in their projections. It addresses the question: What stock market valuations are justified by our expectation of a continuation of New Economy characteristics of rapid productivity growth, low average unemployment coexisting with low average inflation, and mild, infrequent recessions?

Everything that influences stock prices does so through one or more of the following three factors:

- corporate revenue
- profit margins on revenue
- price-earnings (PE) ratios

These three factors may be either anticipated or realized. We shall first examine them on our favorite time horizon—three to five years. Then we will look at them on a ten-to-fifty-year retirement plan horizon.

What is Meant by Investing on a Three-to-Five-Year Time Horizon?

Basically, investing on a three-to-five-year time horizon is a flight from the difficulty of making short-term (a few weeks or months ahead) forecasts of the market. An investor predicts where a stock (or the market) will be in three to five years, but he knows the route for getting there is imponderable. Huge amounts of money can be made by short-term market forecasting by anyone who can do it with reasonable consistency. Most of us cannot do it very well, but we frequently try.

A three-to-five-year time horizon is also a flight from making very long-term forecasts for *individual stocks*.

Technologies and competitive conditions change so rapidly that very long-term forecasts for an individual stock are often difficult to make. Long-term forecasts of the *entire market* are, of course, made for retirement planning.

Short-term forecasting is not ignored, but it usually takes a back seat in making investments for which short-term timing is not crucial. Put another way, the question of the medium-term intrinsic value or earning *power* of a stock (or the market) becomes more important than a forecast of next quarter's or next year's earnings. An investment position taken on a three-to-five-year projection is not set in concrete. Positions are continually reexamined as conditions change and new three-to-five-year projections are made. When a three-to-five-year outlook becomes a bit dubious, short-term projections are frequently made to decide when to liquidate a position.

Long-term trends (longer than five years) are also not ignored when making a three-to-five-year projection. They are considered if the current market is appraised as being far above its very long-term value, as it was in the late 1990s, or far below it, as we believe it was in 2002. An investor can be a lot more confident about buying on a three-to-five-year time horizon if the market is also below *long-term* value estimates.

How Will the Economy Perform in the Next Three to Five Years?

Before making a three-to-five-year forecast of the market, we must make a projection of economic performance for that period.

Pressures to use stimulative monetary and fiscal policy to return the economy to full employment (4 to 4 1/2 percent unemployment rate) will likely be the single most important factor controlling the level of business activity over the coming three to five years. Returning to full employment will require an average real GDP growth rate of about 4 1/2 to 5 percent for three to five years. That is faster than the long-term trend required by the increasing labor force and the productivity growth rate. Political pressures will be strong to achieve that goal, but setbacks may delay complete success by a year or two.

The risk of accelerating inflation poses the greatest danger to the ability of government to achieve full employment in three to five years. The danger of extreme surges in oil prices due to Middle Eastern problems is still haunting us. A possible sudden decline in the dollar on the foreign exchange market would increase import prices. Excessive deficit financing as we approach full employment may be a threat. And for decades the demand for increased social services with inflationary compliance costs as described in Chapter 4 will threaten inflation, to be followed by Federal Reserve restraint and unemployment.

As for the risk of a faltering economy due to inadequate demand, a slowing of consumer spending caused by a leveling off or decline in home prices as mortgage rates rise (described in Chapter 1) is the *single* greatest risk. But if government should adopt the flexible fiscal stimulus plan outlined in Chapter 1, any temporary faltering of demand would not be a serious problem.

Projecting the Corporate Revenue Growth Rate

Corporate revenue is the first of the three factors listed earlier through which all forces that affect stock prices operate. The profit-margin share of these revenues brought down to the bottom line determines the earnings available to stockholders. Then, the price that investors will pay for those earnings is the final determinant of stock prices.

A return to full employment in three to five years will require the creation of about ten million new jobs. It can be done, but, as indicated, it will require an annual growth of *real* GDP of 4 1/2 to 5 percent. That is a full percentage point higher than the long-term trend. Adding an average inflation rate of about 2 1/2 percent will require an annual increase in nominal GDP of about 7 to 7 1/2 percent. *Corporate revenue usually grows just slightly faster than nominal GDP.*

Various potholes such as oil price hikes, terrorist attacks, fluctuating foreign exchange rates, or government-induced impediments to the effectiveness of structural competition to hold down prices may delay recovery, but the pressures to maintain full employment are high, and we expect that goal to be achieved, although perhaps delayed a year or two. Until full employment is reached, above-trend growth can be expected on average.

Projecting Profit Margins on Revenue

How much of that rapidly growing revenue in the coming three to five years will be retained as profit? Chart 9.1 shows historic profit margins *on revenue* for domestic nonfinancial corporations as published in the Survey of Current Business. What can we learn from this chart? Fluctuations have been spectacular and therefore have had an overwhelming impact on short-term changes in corporate profits. This volatility of profit margins makes profit-margin projections both important and difficult.

Chart 9.1 Corporate Profit Margins Per Unit Domestic Nonfinancial Corporations

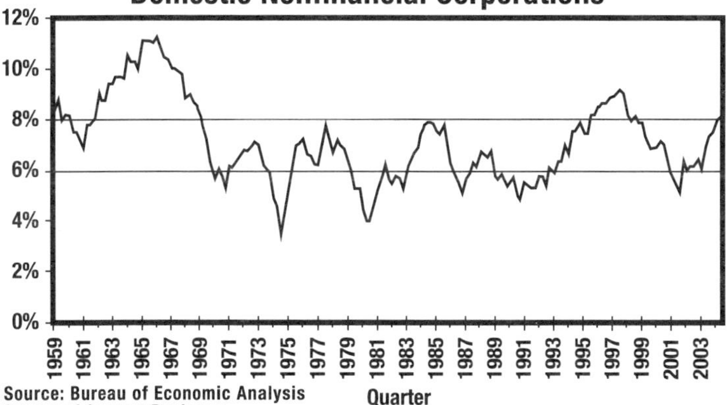

Source: Bureau of Economic Analysis
Survey of Current Business

The great bull market of the 1990s was substantially abetted by an almost 50 percent rise in profit margins from 1993 to 1997. This increase in profit margins, applied to rapidly growing corporate revenues, led to an annual growth in profits for several years of around 15 percent, encouraging widespread absurd forecasts that profits and the stock market would continue to rise at that pace for many years. It was a major factor behind the stock market bubble.

What will profit margins likely be in the coming three to five years? What determines profit margins? Profits are a residual. They are what is left over (a small number) after all costs (a large number) are deducted from revenues (also a large number). Being a residual, profits are knocked about by often unpredictable and uncontrollable changes in all items of revenue and cost involved in a business operation. Small percentage changes in those large numbers can make large percentage changes in the small residual number. Corporate management often requires considerable time to adjust to these changes in revenue and costs in order to achieve their target profit margins. Therefore, profit margins fluctuate widely as economic conditions change.

Of all the *broad* factors that push profit margins around, *capacity utilization and changes in real GDP* are generally most important. Why does capacity utilization affect profit margins? As described in Chapter 3, when output drops farther below capacity, below-capacity competition becomes more vigorous, putting pressure on profit margins. Also, companies are forced to spread fixed costs over the smaller output, thus increasing unit costs and reducing profit margins. As for changes in real GDP, rapid growth makes the maintenance of selling prices above costs easier to achieve, leading to high margins. Costs tend to lag selling prices in periods of rapid growth.

Wall Street analysts frequently use the term *pricing power*. This is a euphemism for the ability to maintain satisfactory profit margins. In 2001–3, reports of the inability to maintain adequate pricing power were almost continuous. This should not be surprising since the two broad factors that usually dominate profit margins were weak—capacity utilization and growth in real GDP. Can we project an *average or normal* level for profit margins appropriate for New Economic conditions?

Is it likely that the high margins well above 8 percent (almost 12 percent at the highest point) shown in the chart for the 1960s can become a *normal* profit margin for the New

Economy? That was an extraordinary period of rapid growth, high capacity utilization (low below-capacity competition), and, through part of the period, *accelerating inflation*. Substantial economic growth will surely continue (perhaps erratically), but if it is accompanied by the extremely low below-capacity competition of that period with its rapid inflation, Federal Reserve inflation-stabilizing policy will quickly kick in, the economy will slow, and profit margins will decline. The very high profit margins of 1963–68 will not likely become an average for the coming years. Much the same can be said for the profit margins slightly above 8 percent in 1996–97. That was also a period of rapid growth in real GDP, but below-capacity competition was significantly stronger (capacity utilization lower) than in the 1960s.

As the chart shows, the other extreme (low profit margins, below 6 percent) has been associated with recessions, very slow growth, and strong below-capacity competition. If we are correct that structural competition will remain strong and that the Federal Reserve, with a bit of help from fiscal authorities, will continue to keep recessions mild and infrequent, we can rule out the possibility of profit margins averaging below 6 percent and confine the expected average profit margin range to between 6 and 8 percent, as it has been for many years. But that is still an unpleasantly wide latitude.

Perhaps that likely two-percentage-point range of expected *average* profit margins can be narrowed a bit. This book has argued that several of the forces underlying New Economy *structural* competition will continue. Therefore, strong structural competition will require less below-capacity competition to restrain inflation, leading to higher profit margins than prevailed in that thirty-year inflation cycle. We suggest that the *average* profit margin for the coming decade or two will be somewhere in the 7-to-8-percent range, using the data supplied in the Survey of Current Business.

Profit margins in late 2004 are near the top of that range. Since the two forces that dominate changes in profit margins—the growth rate of real GDP and capacity utilization—will both be strong (on average) over the coming three to five years, we expect average profit margins to remain high and probably go even a little higher until full employment is reached.

With corporate revenue growing on average at 7 to 7 1/2 percent a year and profit margins on revenue remaining high or even moving up a bit, corporate profits should increase on average about 7 to 9 percent a year for the next three to five years, after which the growth rate will slow moderately. We should note that this average growth rate will be only about half the profit growth rate of 1993 to 1999 that produced the stock market bubble.

Projecting Price-Earnings Ratios

How much will investors pay (*will* pay, not *should* pay) for significantly rising earnings in the coming three to five years? This is the problem of valuation, which is almost always a subject of debate in the financial community, with a wide diversity of opinion.

Some analysts believe the market is now grossly overvalued, but other analysts believe it is fairly valued or even undervalued. Successful investing in the coming three to five years will require a reasonably correct resolution of this perplexing question of what stocks are really worth.

How high a PE ratio will investors pay for expected earnings? It depends on how they judge the future of the economy. If investors come to believe that the economy of the future will look a lot like the Very Old Economy of the first half of the twentieth century with its waves of bank failures, its Great Depression, its major wars, and its breakdown of the international trading system, they will look for guidance to the average PE of that period—a PE of about 13. We do not believe that the history of that Very Old Economy has much to teach us about what we should pay for stocks, and we don't think many other investors will either. Yet the PE experience of that period is included in the average PE for the whole century used for guidance by some investors.

If investors think that the economy of the future will look like that of the Old Economy of the second half of the twentieth century with its thirty-year low-growth, low-productivity inflation cycle, and with socialist dogma and the cold war keeping much of the world in chains for about 80 percent of that period, then they will look for guidance to the average PE of that period—a PE of about 15. We do not believe that that half century has much to tell us about what investors will pay for stocks. We expect that investors will come more and more to believe that improved management of aggregate demand and structural competition (as described in Chapter 3) has created a new and better economy and will continue to develop an even better one. If that is true, investors will be willing to pay a higher price for earnings than investors paid in the past century. After all, the New Economy is only ten or fifteen years old. Although it has been in gestation for many years, it has really gained impetus since the collapse of the Soviet Union (with its near-fatal blow to socialist dogma), with the end of the thirty-year inflation cycle in the United States in the early 1990s, and with the strengthening of structural competition as described in Chapter 3.

If investors are to keep moving toward New Economy stock valuations in the coming three to five years, government will need to maintain New Economy conditions most of the time. If consumer spending should slow due to a leveling off or decline in home prices (or for any other reason), we will need a flexible fiscal stimulus plan to keep aggregate demand growing smoothly. If government should adopt substantial new regulations with increased compliance costs, accelerating inflation will be followed by Federal Reserve restraint and higher unemployment. We must face reality. A continuation of PE ratios above historic patterns depends on the ability of government to manage aggregate demand and structural competition reasonably well. Confidence in that ability will grow only as that ability is demonstrated.

So far we have helped only moderately to unravel the mystery of how much investors will pay for the growing stream of earnings in the coming three to five years. We have claimed only that investors will pay more for earnings than they did in the Very Old Economy of the first half of the twentieth century or the Old Economy of the second half of that century. We hardly need to point out that PE ratios will not likely match the PEs in the high 20s and 30s that prevailed during the bubble years of the late 1990s.

The amount that investors will pay for earnings in the coming three to five years will, of course, depend partly on interest rates on fixed-income obligations—the major alternative investment. Surely interest rates will rise as we approach full employment, but how much? An analysis of the determinants of interest rates must await our discussion of long-term investment for retirement purposes. For the moment we will assume that the yield on the benchmark ten-year Treasury note will rise to about 5 1/2 percent, more than a full percentage point above the present yield.

The so-called Federal Reserve model is probably the most common method of relating interest rates to stock valuation, at least on a short-term basis. It assumes that the *earnings yield* on stocks will tend toward the interest rate yield on ten-year Treasury notes. The earnings yield on stocks is the reciprocal of the PE ratio. A PE ratio of 20 is equivalent to an earnings yield of 5 percent. The higher the PE ratio, the lower the earnings yield. An earnings yield of 5 1/2 percent is equivalent to a PE ratio of about 18.

We have concluded that S&P 500 earnings (currently about $66) will grow about 8 percent on average for the next three to five years. After full employment is reached the growth rate will slow. Therefore, those S&P 500 earnings should reach about $97 in five years. A PE multiple of 18 would make for a price of about 1750 or a 56-percent gain from the present price of about 1120. Better returns will require expert stock selection or profits from intermediate fluctuations. These estimates will certainly be wrong to some extent and perhaps to a considerable extent. But we do not believe they will be as wrong as estimates made by those who are expecting an extended period of below-trend growth or are waiting for a return to Very Old Economy PE ratios in the mid-to-low teens in order to invest. We believe our estimates have been conservative. Our greed prompts us to consider the possibility that as New Economy conditions develop, animal spirits will rise among investors, producing a PE ratio and a market valuation significantly above our projections in the coming three-to-five-year period.

In summary, we are anticipating reasonably intelligent government management of aggregate demand and structural competition over the coming three to five years. If we are wrong in this assessment our stock forecast will also be wrong.

Long-Term Retirement-Type Investing

Employees are usually offered several options as to how their payroll deductions for retirement are to be invested. Those options often include bonds, index funds, large cap stocks, small cap stocks, balanced funds, and even foreign stocks. How is one to choose? We will discuss just one question: Which is the better long-term New Economy investment—stocks or bonds? We will look first at stock investment.

Stock Investment

A long-term chart of the S&P 500 stock average on a ratio scale extended back into the nineteenth century prompts two conclusions: (1) the long-term trend is strongly upward, and (2) price fluctuations are persistent *without any recognizably regular pattern*. The long-term upward trend is due to the fact that the economy grows, and companies take advantage of that growth by reinvesting part or all of their profits in new earning assets, thereby increasing future profits. Persistent fluctuations are due to two facts. First, no one can know the intrinsic value of stocks *within narrow limits* because that value depends on difficult-to-predict future events. Second, price movements in the short term are often based on transitory events and emotional responses. Both the long-term upward trend and the persistent fluctuations are based on those fundamental forces that will continue. Anyone designing a long-term investment plan for retirement must take advantage of the long-term upward trend and protect against (and, if possible, profit from) the persistent fluctuations. Furthermore, such a plan must protect against trading that eats up much of the gains with brokerage fees or other transaction costs. Undue management costs must also be avoided.

A standard dollar-cost-averaging plan can meet these criteria. A regular amount of dollars is invested each month in stocks. More shares are purchased when stock prices are low than when stock prices are high. Over a long period the plan avoids the danger of buying when stocks are popular and selling when they are not. This plan has served well many of the millions of people who have used payroll savings plans for long periods.

Bond Investment

Bond prices have fluctuated widely over the past half century. Chart 9.2 shows interest rates on long-term Treasury

Chart 9.2 Interest Rates on Long-term Treasury Bonds

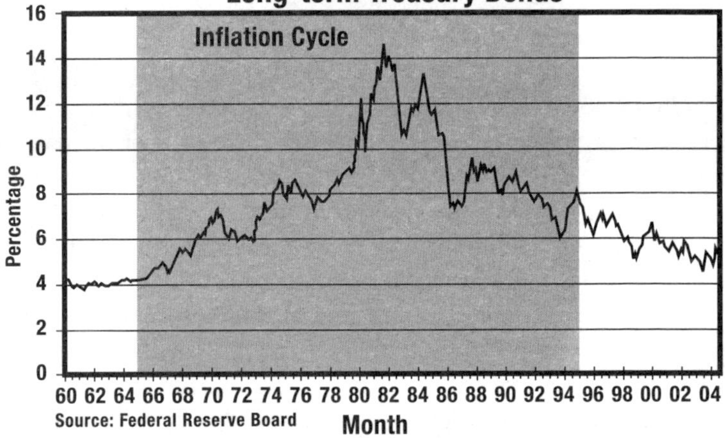

Source: Federal Reserve Board

bonds since 1960. Bond prices fluctuate inversely with changes in current interest rates. As the chart shows, prices have fluctuated widely since 1960, largely due to that long inflation cycle (shown as the shaded area) that began in 1965, peaked in 1980, and ended about 1995. That cycle was due mainly to the faulty management of aggregate demand by the Federal Reserve from 1965 to 1979, which allowed inflation to get out of control. As argued in this book, that will not happen again. Therefore, bond prices will fluctuate in a much narrower range than they have in the past half century. If government should adopt that flexible fiscal stimulus plan described in Chapter 1, highly aggressive interest rate easing by the Federal Reserve in recessions would be avoided and interest rates would fluctuate even less. That would add considerable stability to the economy.

What determines interest rates? Interest rates have two components—a real interest rate to pay the lender for the use of the money and an inflation-risk premium to compensate the lender for a possible loss of purchasing power during the life of the loan. (Corporate bonds also have a premium to cover the risk of default.) Over the last fifty years, fluctuations in the inflation premium have accounted for most of the fluctuations in interest rates. But now that the Federal Reserve (along with most of the world's central banks) has recognized the necessity of keeping inflation low, the inflation premium will be much more stable. It will probably *average* near 2 1/2 percent. The *real* interest rate will, of course, fluctuate over time as the supply and demand for loanable funds on a worldwide basis ebb and flow. We suggest that real interest rates will *average* somewhere near 3 percent. Therefore, we expect the interest rate on ten-year Treasury notes (which has become the benchmark interest rate) to *average* somewhere around 5 1/2 percent, including the inflation premium.

Choosing Between Bonds and Stocks in the New Economy

The balanced fund is an old-fashioned but useful device for investing in *both* bonds and stocks. It helps to protect against (and profit from) fluctuations in both bonds and stocks.

For investors who start with a lump sum, balanced funds are an appropriate way to solve the timing problem. The funds are invested half in stocks and half in bonds. If stocks go up, they become a larger share of the portfolio. When they reach, say, 60 percent of the portfolio, enough stocks are sold and reinvested in bonds to balance the fund. If stocks go down, they become a smaller part of the portfolio. When they are down to, say, 40 percent, bonds are sold and reinvested in stocks to balance the portfolio. This plan forces the investor to sell stocks when they go up and buy them when they drop. Investors on a monthly investment plan would simply add money to that part of the fund that is under 50 percent.

For more aggressive investors, which is the better investment for the long haul in the New Economy, bonds or stocks?

The long-term value of common stocks depends on how fast their earnings will grow. A projection of the growth of stock prices must begin with a projection of the growth rate of the economy. The labor force will likely continue to grow at a rate of around 1 percent a year at least for several years. As projected in Chapter 6, the output per worker hour (productivity) will likely grow at about 2 1/2 to 3 percent a year. Therefore, the real output of the economy will likely grow at about 3 1/2 to 4 percent a year. Inflation should average about 2 1/2 percent a year, yielding a growth rate of *nominal* GDP around 6 to 6 1/2 percent a year. Many unknown factors will surely affect these projected growth rates. Changes in immigration, in the average hours worked each year, or in the retirement age may modify the effective change in labor input. The productivity growth rate and the inflation rate may also be affected by many factors. If errors in each of these projections are additive (all in the same direction) our total projection will be wide of the mark. If several of them are offsetting, our projection of nominal GDP may be fairly close.

We should note that the wildest element of *nominal* GDP has been tamed by the Federal Reserve policy of maintaining stable prices. This is one of the important innovations of the New Economy. We will not experience another inflation surge like that of 1965–80 that produced very rapid growth of *nominal* GDP.

What is the possibility of a prolonged period of *below-potential* growth? As earlier chapters described, we have not yet learned to maintain adequate aggregate demand when monetary stimulation is inadequate as in 2001–4. A flexible fiscal stimulus policy would close that gap. But more worrisome is the fact that we have not fully learned the need to avoid impediments to the ability of structural competition to hold down prices. Inflation, followed by unemployment, is still a threat. We suggest that the learning process will be sufficiently successful to avoid long periods of below-potential growth. Our projection of a 6-to-6 1/2-percent long-term growth in nominal GDP should not be too wide of the mark.

How fast will S&P 500 earnings grow in such an environment? S&P 500 earnings sometimes grow more rapidly than nominal GDP and sometimes more slowly. Not surprisingly, they generally grow more rapidly in periods of rapid economic growth. Consequently, in New Economy conditions we expect S&P 500 earnings to grow about as rapidly as nominal GDP. Many factors affect the relationship between these two growth rates. Most of them are too difficult to project to consider at this time, but one factor should be considered—the dividend payout ratio. For example, in the 1950s, a larger percentage of earnings was paid out as dividends. Consequently, companies were required to issue new stock to finance growth, diluting the old shares and reducing per-share earnings. S&P 500 earnings grew more slowly than nominal GDP. If the reduction in taxes on dividends should encourage substantially greater dividend payouts, S&P 500 earnings would grow at a slower pace. (S&P 500 earnings are reported on a *per share* basis.) But this would be offset by increased dividends, so the total value of stocks would not be affected.

We anticipate that S&P 500 earnings will match the roughly 6-to-6 1/2-percent-a- year growth of nominal GDP over a long period. In addition, stockholders will receive growing dividends amounting to about 1 1/2 percent of the value of stocks held. A 6-to- 6 1/2-percent earnings growth rate plus a 1 1/2-percent dividend would yield the stockholder a total return of 7 1/2 to 8 percent. How would this compare with the likely return on bonds?

We have forecast long-term average interest rates on ten-year Treasury notes of about 5 1/2 percent. Longer-term bonds will likely yield a half percentage point more. Are stocks a better long-term investment than bonds? Our projection of a total return of 7 1/2 to 8 percent on stocks compared to a 6 percent interest return on bonds gives stock ownership a distinct advantage over bonds for a long-term retirement program. However, certain warnings must be raised. A one-and-a-half percentage-point differential between stock and bond yields would be far less than the differential that has prevailed over the last hundred years. The moderate outperformance of stocks could easily be eaten away by transaction costs due to trading or to high management fees. High volatility in stock prices makes stocks less suitable for investment as an individual enters the last ten years before retirement. Tax differences must be considered when investments are not in a tax-free retirement account. *But most important, our forecasts may be wrong.* Anyone who commits *totally* to stock or bond investment is risking a good deal on the accuracy of long-term forecasts.

Stock investment is apparently preferable in a retirement account for those who can handle it, but it is not for everyone. The emotions involved in stock investment could cripple a retirement account for those not qualified to manage it or to select managers to manage it. Anyone who has watched investors over bull and bear markets will attest to the fact that many people fall into that category.

Are Stocks Currently Undervalued on a Long-Term Basis?

As this is written in late 2004, the S&P 500 stock average is about 1120, the approximate average of the last several months. Estimated earnings for the current year are about $66. The PE ratio, then, is about 17. Are stocks undervalued or overvalued? We suggested in our discussion of investing on a three-to-five-year time horizon that medium-term bullish investment judgments are a lot easier to make if stocks are appraised as being undervalued on a long-term basis. If you are wrong on the medium-term, the long-term may help you.

We suggested that stocks are a bit undervalued on a *three-to-five-year time horizon* because growth should be, on average, above trend until we return to full employment. Profit margins, though near the top of the expected long-term average, should remain so (or even go a little higher) for the next three to five years. But what about the very long term? The best way to compare stock investment with bond investment, the only major alternative, is to discount back to the present the flow of expected earnings and dividends on stocks, and the expected interest income on bonds. We have projected a long-term growth rate on S&P 500 earnings of about 6 to 6 1/2 percent and also a continuing dividend yield of about 1 1/2 percent or a total return of about 7 1/2 to 8 percent. We have also projected an average interest rate on long-term Treasury bonds of 6 percent.

If a true long-term investor assumes that these differential returns between stocks and bonds will actually materialize *for a great many years*, a PE ratio far above the present 17 would be warranted, perhaps 30 or 40. Buying stock at the present 17 multiple would produce a far higher return over fifty years than a 6-percent return on bonds. But high PEs have a built-in correction factor. High PEs induce corporations to issue new stock to buy new productive assets. As productive capacity increases, below-capacity competition intensifies, profit margins decline, and so do stock prices. Also, high PEs induce managements to issue stock to buy other companies, employees, debt instruments, and almost anything, thus diluting the per-share earnings and eventually bringing about a correction of stock prices. High PE ratios turn stock certificates into a kind of cash that managements love to spend to build their empires. That is the story of what happened in the late 1990s.

Are stocks (in late 2004) somewhat undervalued on a very long-term basis? For those with the mental discipline to handle the emotional problems, we think they are. Are stocks somewhat undervalued on a three-to-five-year time horizon? We think they are. Are stocks undervalued on a six-to-twelve-*month* time horizon? We haven't a clue.

The Long View of Investment—And the Economy

In this discussion of investment, we have emphasized the uncertainties involved in making financial forecasts. Many things can go wrong. But this book as a whole has emphasized the important aspects of the New Economy that are likely to go *right*. The governments of the world will be forced by competition and the need to modernize to adopt those wonderful policies described in Chapter 7 that are necessary to attract capital investment. The changing nature and intensity of competition among private producers on a globalized basis will ensure a long-term acceleration of knowledge discovery and invention, leading to improved productivity and much greater wealth more evenly distributed among countries. The monetary authorities will be forced by suspicious bond investors to maintain a reasonably effective anti-inflation policy.

Of course, the path toward a globalized, competitive New Economy will not be smooth. The bumps and potholes along the way will make many wonder at times if we have lost our way. Hopes and fears induced by these bumps and potholes will be exaggerated in volatile financial markets, providing enticing opportunities for those with the mental discipline to see the emotional swings for what they are.

END NOTES

[1] Federal Reserve Board, *Federal Open Market Committee Meeting Transcripts*, September 24, 1996, Washington D.C. See also *Federal Open Market Committee Meeting Transcripts*, December 17, 1996.

[2] See for example Robert J. Shiller, "Margin Calls: Should the Fed Step In? Yes, It May Avert Disaster," *Wall Street Journal*, April 10, 2000.

[3] William G. Shepherd, "Causes of Increased Competition in the U.S. Economy, 1939-80," *The Review of Economics and Statistics*, November 1982.

[4] Ronald Reagan, *Address to the Nation on the Program for Economic Recovery*, September 24, 1981; Ronald Reagan, *Remarks Announcing the Establishment of the National Commission on Social Security Reform*, December 16, 1981.

[5] This classification of countries was adapted from World Bank and Oxford University Press, *Globalization, Growth, and Poverty: Building an Inclusive World Economy*, 2002. See also *The Economist*, "Special Report on Globalization," February 2, 2002, p. 66.

[6] Alfred D. Stafford, "Is the Rate of Invention Declining?" *The American Journal of Sociology*, May 1956.

[7] Part of this discussion of the organization of R&D was adapted from Herbert I. Fusfeld, *Industry's Future: Changing Patterns of Industrial Research*, Washington D.C., American Chemical Society, 1994.

[8] Hernando DeSoto, *The Mystery of Capital,* New York, Basic Books, 2000.

[9] Fareed Zakaria, *The Future of Freedom*, New York, W. W. Norton, 2003.